Contradictions

in

COLLABORATION

New Thinking
on
School/University Partnerships

THE EDUCATORS FOR COLLABORATIVE CHANGE

Primary Authors
Tom Adams
Mary Kathleen Barnes
Reba Bricher
Mary Christenson
Don Cramer
Rosario Galarza
Paul Green
Marilyn Hawk
Kathy Iböm
Richard M. Kerper
Kathy Nalle
Daa'iyah Saleem
J. Michael Thomas
Jean Tingley
Cynthia Tyson
Donna Weatherholtz
Lisa Westhoven
Sue Wightman
Charlene Williams

Contributing Authors
Brenda Ambrose
Kathy Barkhurst
Amy Campbell
Lisa Cline
Kathy Davenport
Sue Knuebel
Bill Lohr

\ *Contradictions*
in
COLLABORATION /

New Thinking
on
School/University Partnerships

MARILYN JOHNSTON
WITH THE EDUCATORS FOR COLLABORATIVE CHANGE

FOREWORD BY MAXINE GREENE

Teachers College, Columbia University
New York and London

Published by Teachers College Press, 1234 Amsterdam Avenue, New York, NY 10027

The lines from "Cartographies of Silence" are from *The Dream of a Common Language: Poems 1974-1977* by Adrienne Rich. Copyright © 1978 by W. W. Norton & Company, Inc. Reprinted by permission of the author and W. W. Norton & Company, Inc.

Library of Congress Cataloging-in-Publication Data
Johnston, Marilyn A.
     Contradictions in collaboration : new thinking on
   school/university partnerships / Marilyn A. Johnston with The
   Educators for Collaborative Change ; foreword by Maxine Greene.
          p.   cm.
   Includes bibliographical references and index.
   ISBN 0-8077-3657-0. — ISBN 0-8077-3656-2 (pbk.)
     1. College-school cooperation—Ohio—Longitudinal studies.
   I. Educators for Collaborative Change.   II. Title.
   LB2331.53.J64   1997
   378.1'03—dc21   97-17506

ISBN 0-8077-3656-2 (paper)
ISBN 0-8077-3657-0 (cloth)
Printed on acid-free paper
Manufactured in the United States of America

03 02 01 00 99 98 97   8 7 6 5 4 3 2 1

Contents

Foreword

A community, wrote John Dewey (1954),

> ... presents an order of energies transmuted into one of meanings which are appreciated and mutually referred by each to every other on the part of those engaged in combined action. ... The work of conversion of the physical and organic phase of associated behavior into a community of action saturated and regulated by mutual interest in shared meanings, consequences which are translated into ideas and desired objects by means of symbols, does not occur all at once nor completely. At any given time, it sets a problem rather than marks a settled achievement. (pp. 153–154)

The "combined action" in this book, and the pursuit of "shared meanings" are enacted by means of a process of collaboration between members of a university faculty, public school teachers, graduate students, and researchers. Here, too, given all the tensions and the differences, there can be no "settled achievement." The multiple authors and participants offer their discoveries as possibilities for their readers; they want them to be provocative in the various voices in which they are expressed. They do not want them to be taken as generalizable answers or solutions to all the problems facing teacher education and the schools.

Because of the differences among the participants and the diverse perspectives that mark what they say and do, the book reads like a play in many places. Indeed, one way of encountering it is by imagining a large, open stage with distinctive persons moving in and out, grouping themselves variously, articulating who they are by the nature of their participation in the dialogues that make up the content of the play. If we do use this metaphor, we cannot but help note how this playing out of collaboration is like contemporary theatre. Details of human transactions that we normally would not notice become viable; frequencies ordinarily unheard become audible.

One reason for this is that the various participants, whether from the university, the public school, or the parent body, are encouraged to reflect on what they trying to bring into being as they work together. Marilyn Johnston, who was the initiator of this work and (for all the difficulty of confronting it) the director of the play, continually asks herself questions about her relation to the hierarchies she is trying to overcome, about the tensions between the discourses in use, even about the ethics of deciding what could be said and what could not. She is sharply aware, as are her colleagues, of the interpretive stance she and others are taking: What they find out and what they want to accomplish where professional development is concerned are dependent on the ways they "read" the classroom and seminar room scenes in which they are involved.

At a time when we are at last coming to terms with diversity and with the capacities of teachers to collaborate with one another in the choices they make, this book takes on a unique importance. Realizing that the fiction of the autonomous teacher free to make her own decisions behind a closed door can no longer be sustained, the authors take the risk of presenting the intricacies and contradictions and, yes, the pleasures of the collaborative process at a moment when old hierarchies and top–down supervisions have been exposed. They are, indirectly at least, proposing to their readers that they do something as daring as they did when they decided—in all their difference— to write a book together. Remarkable and courageous as that decision was, it is what makes the book so fascinating and so generative. Personal differences are revealed; cultural differences (as in the case of conversation by two African-American women) are examined. The crucial linkages between reflection and communication, reflection and planning, planning and conversation all promise transformations in the schools. Since the locale is largely Columbus, Ohio, which paid special attention to the quincentenary anniversary of Columbus's voyage to this hemisphere, the authors seized the opportunity to show how collaboration worked with regard to concrete projects, even problematic ones that demanded reflection by an entire community. Again, the risks were many; the tensions, in time, were a source of creativity.

We are reminded once more of the range of differences among teachers and their personal histories; and we are reminded as well of the importance of role when it comes to transactions, say, among academic scholars and practicing teachers. Somehow, even without a triumphant conclusion, the writers weave a tale of increasing care among the teachers and increasing mutuality. This book becomes an exemplar of a community in the making, which is one of the ways in which democracy is described. We are left in a kind of wonderful uncertainty, challenged to explore collaboration in our multiple contexts. Altered experiences of scholarship and teaching may lie ahead.

—*Maxine Greene*

REFERENCE

Dewey, J. (1954). *The public and its problems*. Athens, OH: Swallow Press.

Acknowledgments

I have many acknowledgments to make. The first is to my PDS colleagues.

Classroom Teachers
Dee Azbell
Sandie Barthelmas
Shirley Bendau
Melba Bias
Belva Buchan
Sue Burt
Karen Caw
Mary Collins
Ann Dote
Francee Eldredge
Geri Granger
Carol Helm
Lori Hoffman
Judy Hubin
Debbie Jester
Mike Johnson
Marilyn Karl
Doris Los
Debbie Mancus
Jenny Newton
Kim Perry
Linda Safford
Alan Snow
Linda Sticklan
Erica Todarello
Sarah Van Horn
Amy Webster
Renee White

School Principals
Susan Barker
Joe Copeland
Paul Jones
Kay Noble
Todd Rogers

Graduate Associates
Rhonda Burke-Spero
Denise Dallmer
Floyd Funderburg
Christy Glaser
JoAnn Hohenbrink
Anke Knecht
Isaac Larison
Susi Long
Mary Shorey

OSU *Faculty*
Michael Beeth
Connie Bowman
Terry Herrera
Don Williams
Anita Woolfolk-Hoy
Jerry Zutell

Without them I would have had little worth saying about school/university collaboration. From them I have learned much more than I anticipated and more than I could capture in this book.

The authors want to thank the readers of their chapters for feedback and support: chapter 1, Judy Hubin and Sue Wightman; chapter 2, J. Michael Thomas and Jerry Zutell; chapter 3, J. Michael Thomas and Lisa Westhoven; chapter

4, Karen Caw and Judy Hubin; chapter 5, Carol Helm and Lisa Westhoven; chapter 6, Kathleen Ibom and Lisa Westhoven; chapter 7, J. Michael Thomas; chapter 8, Cynthia Smith and Renee White; chapter 9, Mary Christenson.

I also want to thank Michael Parsons, whose loving support kept me going and whose persistent feedback kept me rethinking and rewriting; Maxine Greene, who was my first woman mentor and who gave me my first aspirations to be a scholar; my women colleagues in the Post-Modern Study (PMS) group, who keep me unsettled and uncomfortable with easy conclusions; and Juana Sancho and Fernando Hernandez, who lent us their *casa de fin de semana* (weekend house) in a quiet medieval village outside Barcelona, Spain—the tranquillity and country walks did much to support the writing of this book.

—*Marilyn Johnston*

Introduction

This is a book about collaboration, written collaboratively. It is based on a six-year longitudinal study of our collaboration in a professional development school (PDS) project at The Ohio State University. We use our experiences in the PDS to examine the issues and challenges of school/university collaboration.

This is not a tidy tale; collaboration is an untidy business, full of uncharted territories, ambiguities, and institutional complexities. Our goal is to describe this complexity and question our collaborative experience as well as disrupt the wider, often uncritical, use of collaboration in the education literature. We speak in many voices—as classroom teachers, principals, doctoral students, and university faculty. We try not to mask our differences or difficulties with texts or conclusions that are more coherent than our experiences. On the other hand, we are excited by what we have learned and by the collegial relationships that support our continuing professional development.

We are a group of about 45 educators who teach at eight elementary and middle schools (in the Columbus and Worthington school districts) and a university (The Ohio State University). Teachers and principals from the schools and faculty and doctoral students from the university work together to plan, implement, and evaluate a master's of education program for a yearly cohort of 35 graduate-level preservice teachers. Our professional development school, the Educators for Collaborative Change (ECC), began in May 1991, and we have been meeting weekly as a group for six years to develop goals and instigate change. We have four primary goals: (1) reform in teacher education, (2) professional development, (3) inquiry, and (4) urban education. These are not separate goals, but integrated ones.

This book has two parts. The first looks at issues and problems in collaboration. Chapter 1 lays the groundwork for the three primary ideas—differences, tensions, and dialogue—that shape our understandings in this book. Chapter 2 gives an overall history of the project from my point of view. Chapter 3 uses an incident at our first research presentation to raise issues about the role of the individual in collaborative groups. In chapter 4, Rick Kerper, a doctoral student, and I (as university participants) examine the ways we changed our minds about our roles and positionings within this collaborative project. In chapter 5, two African American participants in our PDS raise questions from their cultural situatedness about collaboration as it emerged in this PDS. Chapter 6 presents school-based voices and stories related to a wide range of issues—the confusion of a new participant, a cooperating teacher's reflection on journaling with her intern, a principal's perspective on collaboration, and the experience of collaborative teaching in a third-grade classroom. Chapter 7 is a chapter on the theoretical and methodological positions that influenced my own work in the project and on this book.

Between the chapters in part I, the reader will find brief sections titled "Interlude With a Metaphor." We often use metaphors in the PDS as a way to extend and provoke our thinking. Some participants have developed their metaphors in written form. These reflect how they worked in practice. Metaphors emerged when it was difficult to explain something without them. At other times a metaphor helped an individual or group to work through a provocative point or problem. Metaphors were seldom the topic of discussion, but rather, worked as an intermittent tool to elaborate, explain, and/or extend ideas.

You will also see occasional inserts in the text labeled "Academic Aside." These academic discussions are set off from regular text by a different typeface. They are highlighted in this way so that readers not interested in more academic discussions can pass them by, and those who wish to can locate them more easily.

Part II focuses on the results of our initial research project to study collaboration as it developed. Two case studies compare the way collaboration developed in two PDS schools. Chapters 8 and 9 are written by teachers as they documented the challenges of collaboration in their particular school contexts. There are sharp contrasts between these two cases (one urban, one suburban) as well as provocative similarities.

Throughout the book, authors for each chapter are listed alphabetically; some authors chose to use pseudonyms. Author biographical sketches, except for those using pseudonyms, are found at the end of the book.

We expect that our readers will be as diverse as we are and suggest below several ways to read this book. It is possible to read it from cover to cover, but we have also tried to write the chapters as independent units so that readers can select and choose chapters (and sections of chapters) depending on their interests. Within chapters, we also reference other places where similar issues are discussed.

We suggest several ways to read:

- For considerations of collaboration and the practical implications of developing a PDS, see chapters 2, 4, 8, and 9.
- For the theoretical issues that grounded this project, see chapters 1, 5, and 7.
- For a historical look at the project, see chapters 2, 3, and 4.
- For school-based perspectives on this project, see chapters 6, 8, and 9.

We use a lot of acronyms and titles in our project. We employ these as sparingly as possible, but it is difficult to write without them and cumbersome to write out names and titles repeatedly. The following are used here.

CE: *Clinical educator.* A classroom teacher who is released from classroom teaching responsibilities to work with the PDS. One CE is full-time at the university, a second is released half-time to co-coordinate the PDS, and several teachers are released one day a week to work in their school buildings.

CT: *Cooperating teacher, collaborating teacher.* A teacher in the PDS who works with our MEd interns.

GA: *Graduate associate.* Doctoral-level student at the university who has an assistantship to work in the PDS. GAS roles are varied but include working collaboratively with school clinical educators to supervise MEd interns, co-teaching methods courses, writing grant proposals, conducting inquiry and action research projects, and participating in conference presentations and writing projects.

INTERN: *MEd student.* A post-baccalaureate student seeking elementary and middle school certification in a five-quarter master's of education program in our PDS.

PDS: *Professional development school.* A school or group of teachers and administrators from several schools who come together to do PDS work. At Ohio State University, there are presently 11 PDSs. Ours, the Educators for Collaborative Change, has four primary goals: reform in teacher education, professional development, inquiry and urban education.

GA/CE MEETING: Meeting held weekly with graduate associates, clinical educators, and university faculty to discuss problems, talk about issues, and plan for our Thursday night meetings.

THURSDAY MEETING: Meeting held each Thursday after school for the group to make decisions about PDS issues and problems, plan and share inquiry projects, and develop and evaluate our MEd program.

There are multiple authors in this book in order to represent, however partially, our diversity. To do this, we frame the book around some understandings of three broad themes—differences, tensions, and dialogue—that evolved in the group context. These reflect the struggles we have encountered working across the differences that emerged from our grounding in different institutional contexts. We try to make our differences explicit. To do this we write in many voices and make distinctions between our different *voices, perspectives,* and *experiences.* We use the term *voice* to mean individual interpretations of experience and a point of view. This includes the style and manners in which individuals express themselves and the choice of things they reveal. We use *perspective* for larger organizing worldviews—in Senge's terms, "mental models" (1990). These include our assumptions, both those we are aware of and those we are not. Both voice and perspective we understand to be influenced by social learning. We write about the *experiences* we have had together, but not as a single experience, for we often had different experiences even when we were at the same event. Our goal is to represent as well and as explicitly as we can what we have learned from these experiences in ways that reflect multiple voices and perspectives.

We do not expect what we have learned to be generalizable, and in order to contextualize them we deliberately situate our ideas in particular experiences and individual perspectives. We do anticipate, however, that they will be useful by comparison for those planning for or working on collaborative projects.

Our collaboration to write this book worked at several levels. At its most basic, what we have learned together is the ubiquitous ground on which the book rests. Selected aspects of what we learned are here in writing. Some stories are omitted here because their authors either did not choose to write them or didn't have the time; other stories are omitted because of their sensitive personal or political character. The book, however, rests on all these experiences—whether articulated or not.

A second level of collaboration occurred as people worked together to write, to give others feedback on their writing, and to encourage the persistence it takes to get a piece ready for publication. Those who provided substantive feedback and encouragement are listed in the Acknowledgments.

My roles in constructing this book are complicated. I wrote the proposal and then pushed the idea of this book when few were initially interested or believed it possible. As a university-based participant, I have professional motives for this kind of publishing, and I had a sabbatical leave that supported the writing. I have been troubled from the beginning about encouraging school-based participants to write because they are given neither time, nor support, nor rewards for doing so. I persevered nevertheless, both because many who did write found it rewarding and helpful to their learning, and because I did not want to tell my version without including those of others, written as they wanted to represent themselves. I acknowledge, however, my influence during the writing and editing processes in all aspects of this book.

Many individual voices and pieces would no doubt have developed differently if someone else had been nurturing them.

Some individual autonomy on the teachers' part, however, is evident because the book looks much different than I had anticipated. I initially planned for a book that would show different perspectives around some central issues where we both agreed and disagreed across institutional boundaries. The diversity turned out to be of a different kind. Authors have written about the things they cared about, which were not always related to my themes, and in ways that reflected their personalities and writing styles. Consequently, our differences do not get articulated as directly as I had initially wanted nor are they organized thematically in ways I would have preferred. Most participants choose to write about their experiences. The results are richly textured details and narratives more than themes and issues. I realize in retrospect that I naively expected discussions of general themes in order to draw conclusions, which I now see as impossible. What we provide instead of conclusions are descriptions of what we have learned from the challenges of trying to do school/university collaboration.

Some authors felt both personal and political risk in articulating these challenges explicitly in their writing. Therefore, the good, bad, and the ugly are expressed at whatever levels individuals felt safe with. I personally push these issues somewhat harder, and (with their feedback) have written about them from my perspective.

Throughout the writing for this book I have struggled with pronoun use. On the one hand, I recognize my editorship and authority throughout the book and use "I" to indicate when I am most clearly situated in this position. At other times, even though I am acutely aware that there are representational problems in speaking "for" or even "with" others (Visweswaran, 1994), I use a plural pronoun to indicate where my own thinking has so clearly evolved from our "group thinking" that I am hesitant to claim it as "my" interpretation. As both a participant and a researcher in this project, I find the representational issues endless, problematic, and intriguing. (See chapter 7 for further discussions on these topics.)

Collaboration is made more complex by the relational requirements of this kind of work. Collaboration is dependent on relationships and communication. It has ups and downs, misunderstandings, and challenges, like any person-to-person endeavor. Collaboration also requires attention to the moral and ethical aspects of those relationships, for example, the demands of caring (Noddings, 1984), the issues of voice and identity (Britzman, 1991), the ethical problems of doing research while building relationships with participants (Oakley, 1981), and the problems raised by racial, sexual, and class boundaries (hooks, 1994).

In this project, a collaborative process has supported change in programs, teaching, and individual/group thinking far beyond our initial expectations. Most of us have found this kind of collaboration much more supportive of critical reflection and growth than other kinds of reform and professional development projects of which we have been a part. At the same time, we are less optimistic that school/university collaboration can survive institutional constraints and political pressures for cost-effective change. We are thus pessimistic even as we are convinced that this kind of collaboration leads to the kind of sustainable change that both educators and politicians claim is needed.

We have learned much about our collaboration, both the struggles and the rewards, from writing this book. We invite you to use what we have learned to provoke your own thinking about the complex issues related to school/university collaboration.

Issues and Challenges of Collaboration

In part I we focus on the history and development of collaboration in our professional development school (PDS). In the beginning, there was a sense of fragility and ambiguity to our efforts. None of us had a clear vision of how collaboration should best work across the traditional differences that have separated schools and universities. Our primary commitment was to do something different, to take reform in teacher education seriously, and to reconstruct our relationships in ways that were less hierarchical and demeaning to school-based participants. Traditionally, university-based knowledge and roles have held higher prestige and been ascribed higher value. We understood collaboration as commonality of purpose and equality of power relations, but we were hard pressed to define exactly what this might look like in practice.

Initially we tended to romanticize these requirements of commonality and especially equality in ways that made it difficult for university participants to exercise leadership, even though they were initiating the project. We disenfranchised university-based participants in order to empower school-based participants. School-based participants, however, were hesitant because they did not trust what was being said and they had had no part in setting the original agenda. Moving from traditional roles to the relationships and dialogue necessary to support mutuality and equality was uncharted territory for us all. Issues of power and relationships permeated much of what we did in the early years. What we learned from this is the focus of the first part of the book.

We follow these early ideas through transitions in our thinking and practices. We constructed new ways of thinking about our differences and new ways of talking across them. We slowly came to new understandings of collaboration and shared goals that led us in unanticipated directions. We initially thought about our differences as a source of conflict and later came to understand how these differences were a firm foundation for our continued learning. We initially thought university-based participants had to give up their power in order to empower school-based participants and later found dialogue to be a means of creating more fluid positionings and mutual relationships.

This is not a linear story with a happy ending. It is more like a continuous reconstruction of ideals and relationships with no clear end in sight. By and large it has been an enormously rewarding journey, but it has required endurance and perseverance. We hope our insights lend support to those in the midst of similar struggles and that our multivoiced, multiperspectival account conveys the complexity of reform initiatives as well as the personal sacrifices and institutional support necessary to sustain them.

CHAPTER 1

Keeping Differences in Tensions Through Dialogue

Marilyn Johnston and J. Michael Thomas

Three ideas shape the theoretical frame of this book—differences, tensions, and dialogue. The *differences* between schools and universities are well documented. The tensions created by these differences, when school and university people try to collaborate, are also well known. In this chapter we trace the rethinking of our differences. We move from thinking about differences as potentially conflictful to situating them in *productive tensions*. The means to this transition was *dialogue*. For us, dialogue involves a particular way of talking about and learning from our differences. Differences kept in tension in a dialogue nurture critique and learning.

The ideas of *differences*, *tensions*, and *dialogue* are central to the work of our PDS. Put simply, our most significant learning seems to emerge out of dialogic efforts to surface and explore the tensions related to our differences. But as the quotations below suggest, these ideas are complex and fluid.

A dialectical relation marks every human situation: it may be the relation between individual and the environment, self and society, or living consciousness and object-world. Each such relation presupposes a mediation and a tension between the reflective and material dimensions of lived situations. Because both dimensions are equally significant, the tension cannot be overcome by a triumph of subjectivity or objectivity; the dialectic cannot finally be resolved. (Greene, 1995, p. 52)

The central purpose [of dialogue] is to establish a field of genuine meeting and inquiry—a setting in which people can allow a free flow of meaning and vigorous exploration of the collective background of their thought, their personal predispositions, the nature of their shared attention, and the rigid features of their individual and collective assumptions. (Isaacs, 1993, p. 25)

As the theoretical and performative aspects of our three working themes—differences, tensions, and dialogue—interact, our understanding of them and the relations between them change. In time they may lose their usefulness. For now, however, these ideas sustain a lively dialogue.

DIFFERENCES IN PRODUCTIVE TENSIONS

Our present understanding of tensions developed out of struggles to deal with our differences. These differences between schools and universities are well documented (Collins, 1995; Darling-Hammond, 1994; Haberman, 1971; Petrie, 1995; Sirotnik & Goodlad, 1988; Symonds, 1958). More often than not, these differences are represented as the cause of conflict and are sometimes the demise of collaborative projects (Heckman, 1988; Stoddart, 1995). In this book you will find many references to our differences and to how various participants have understood and dealt with the challenges presented by them.

Our differences were difficult to talk about because we thought about them as dichotomies that carried normative values of good and bad. Most of us assumed that discussing these differences would cause conflict, and conflict seemed antithetical to collaboration. In order to avoid conflict, we tried to resist claims that one teaching approach or set of assumptions was better than another. But of course, all of us were committed to certain points of view and made private value judgments. No doubt the "power position" of the university meant that some ideas carried more "authority" than others. One likely effect was to silence teachers with different points of view.

> *Marilyn:* When I began this project, I had read about the differences and potential conflicts between schools and universities. I thought my 15 years as a classroom teacher would help me bridge these differences. It did not take me long to see how naive these attitudes were. I was initially a "role," not a person. I came from the university, and because the teachers did not know me otherwise, [to them] I was a representative of a stereotype.
>
> My reaction to this realization was to tread softly. I thought that if we talked about our differences too overtly they would get in the way of peaceful coexistence. I also thought that if we constructed enough shared perspectives, the differences would go away. But of course they did not, and the most important differences were the most difficult to talk about.

While we typically avoided talking directly about our differences, we talked endlessly in abstract ways about what to do about them. We were aware that many collaborative projects had disbanded because people could not deal with their differences. We hoped to avoid this but did not know how.

School/University Differences in the Literature

Researchers writing about collaboration have used a number of concepts and ideas—tensions, dilemmas, dualisms, dialectics, dichotomies—to describe the differences between schools and universities. This literature helped us make some distinctions and consider various approaches to dealing with differences.

ACADEMIC ASIDE: REVIEW OF THE LITERATURE

Some authors in this literature on school/university differences focus on describing the differences without theorizing about them. For example, Miller (1995) discusses the "thorny issues" or "tensions" (centralization versus decentralization, university versus school cultures, theoretical versus craft knowledge) that occurred in the collaboration of 25 school districts with the University of Southern Maine. Nancy Winitsky, Trish Stoddart, and Patti O'Keefe (1992) describe a number of "dilemmas" that occurred in their school/university collaboration, including collaboration versus academic freedom, didactic versus constructivist views of teaching, replicative versus reflective orientation, and basic versus applied research.

Some researchers emphasize the inevitability of difference and the consequences for reform initiatives that attempt to break down the traditional isolation of schools and universities. Lampert (1991) argues:

> institutional reorganizations will not erase the tensions that have always existed between research and practice, between teaching as a profession and formal teacher education, and between researchers and teacher educators. These tensions will simply move from the institutional level to the level of the individuals who are trying to fill the boundary-blurring roles that restructured institutions create. (p. 674)

Most traditional organizational arrangements keep professionals in their separate institutional cultures, where they seldom experience tensions firsthand. Lampert's point is that restructuring puts some of these people, the "boundary spanners," in positions where they are directly confronted with differences and their inherent tensions.

Rather than accept their inevitability, some authors argue that it is necessary to resolve tensions. Knight, Wiseman, and Smith (1992) argue for resolving the "reflectivity-activity dilemma" which characterizes school and university orientations. With a similar orientation, Henderson and Hawthorne (1995) argue that collaborative groups must move from university dominance to shared power, from individualistic practices to community-grounded ones, from technical teaching to co-constructivist teaching, and from reductionistic achievement measures to long-term qualitative evaluation. Moving from traditional school/university orientations to a new set of assumptions is one way to resolve the difference. Another approach to resolving tensions is to embrace them. Elbow (1986) recommends "embracing contraries" in an internal dialectic that eventually leads to "new and larger frames of reference" (p. 251).

Zeichner (1991) represents a group of researchers who see differences as a way to work toward social reform. He proposes a democratic model to integrate differences between communities and schools. A democratic community "recognizes the legitimate rights of all parties to have substantive input into decision making" (p. 371). In this approach, differences contribute to a dialogue where all interests are represented. For Zeichner, differences and tensions are necessary to equity and social reform.

Overall, in the research literature there seem to be two general approaches to dealing with school/university differences. One group primarily describes the differences that caused conflicts in their collaborative projects. A second argues for resolving the tensions by creating a wider view or a new synthesis. Initially we saw the differences between schools and universities as potential sites of conflict; we conclude with the position that tensions cannot be resolved and are instead to be cherished as potential sites for our learning and growth.

In our rethinking of our differences, we were heavily influenced by John Dewey (1916). Dewey consistently worked with dualisms and their interrelatedness. He typically first described the differences between two aspects of a dichotomy and then argued for their relatedness. For example, one such dichotomy—the individual and the community—relates directly to collaboration. For Dewey, the individual both is created by the community and influences its directions. To sacrifice the individual to the community limits the potential of the individual's growth; on the other hand, to move too far in the direction of individual rights limits the potential of the community's growth. The reciprocity of the individual and the community, for Dewey, is always in need of negotiation and adjustments. This negotiation depends heavily on the individual's social interaction within the community.

> To learn to be human is to develop through the give-and-take of communication an effective sense of being an individually distinctive member of a community; one who understands and appreciates its beliefs, desires, and methods, and who

contributes to a further conversion of organic powers into human resources and values. But this transition is never finished. (Dewey, 1984/1927, p. 332)

For Dewey, this interaction of the individual within the community was productive and democratic only when learning occurred—both individual and group learning. The idea of learning from tensions was an emerging idea that guided our reconstruction in thinking about differences.

Dewey's idea of social negotiation in the shaping and learning of a community underlies our interest in working across differences in productive ways. Rather than theorizing our way into this new approach to dealing with differences, our theories grew out of examining our practices and learning from the problems that arose from our interactions. This learning from experience is straightforwardly a Deweyan approach.

Practice Informs Theorizing

Our rethinking was fueled by what we were learning from our differences. We frequently found that our most potent learning situations grew out of conversations where our differences were most evident. We talked about the character of these conversations and agreed that learning was occurring because of, not in spite of, our differences.

When we agreed, there were few challenges to our thinking. When there were differences, we had to reflect, compare, and adjust our thinking in light of someone else's perspective. When our differences exist in this kind of productive tension, learning is most likely to occur. But this kind of learning is costly. It almost always involves confronting aspects of ourselves that are hidden or unacknowledged; it usually leaves us searching for who we are. Living in tension is living in ambiguity. Our institutions often are not supportive of or receptive to this kind of social and slowly evolving meaning making.

Talking About Tensions. In this interpretation of tensions, we assume a necessary relationship between differences. Rather than understanding differences as potential sites of conflict, we look for their interrelatedness. Like the north and south Poles of a magnet, the differences interact in ways that make them interdependent. Both are necessary if things are going to hold together. In teacher education, for example, theory and practice are often separate and in conflict. Theory is seen as the bastion of the university (for example, in teacher education coursework) and practice is considered the purview of schools (as with student teaching). Coursework and student teaching are done by different sets of people, who often arrive with different orientations. This obscures the necessary relationship of theory and practice.

To keep them in tension is to look for their relatedness, anticipating not that they will merge but that they will create a richer interaction.

Tensions in Collaboration. Collaboration is teeming with tensions. As we started to look for them, they were everywhere.

> *Marilyn:* I had the same experience reading Lakoff and Johnson's book *Metaphors We Live By* [1980]. As they suggest, metaphors are structured into language in ways that make them invisible until you start to recognize them. It was like that with tensions. There were tensions in everything we did. For example, hierarchy has been an issue for us as a group and especially for me. I tried initially to get rid of it, which did not work. Using tensions as a frame of reference, I later came to see hierarchy and collaboration as complementary parts of our work. We live in institutional and conceptual hierarchies. When we make choices, we do so in relation to moral, intellectual, social, and other kinds of hierarchies. Our charge in these instances is not to abandon hierarchy. Rather, we look for ways to use hierarchical power while simultaneously searching for its abuses and the ways we may ourselves be complicit in sustaining them.

In school/university collaborations, we live in the tensions between hierarchy and mutuality. When we lean too heavily in favor of hierarchy, we lose a sense of mutuality; when we lean too far in the other direction, we tend toward too much ambiguity. For some purposes, however, we need more hierarchy or more mutuality to accomplish the task. Such choices are not clean or easy. There are forms of hierarchy that lead to domination and control, and other hierarchies that allow for shared leadership and work. There are forms of mutuality where people are silenced for fear of disturbing the goodwill of the group as well as mutuality that supports and challenges us.

> *Mike:* When we first began to talk about tensions, I decided to put the idea to work in my role as our PDS ethnographer. At the end of the fourth year, we did a round of interviews with everyone in the PDS. I grouped responses around some of the tensions I saw in the interviews, pointing to the range of ideas, opinions, and beliefs, and passed them out to the group. This concrete representation of some of our differences provided an occasion to talk about and celebrate what characterized us as a group. My objective was to validate our differences as positive aspects within a range of tensions [for a sample of some of these tensions, see Figure 1]. Of course, talking about differences in this way does not make it so. Not everyone felt the same kind

of appreciation, and some were no doubt disturbed by this articulation of our differences. I have also come to doubt some of the distinctions that I made. Too many of them carry baggage that prompts resolution rather than inquiry. For example, there isn't really a tension between empowerment and disempowerment. Most would choose to be empowered rather than disempowered. A real tension must be one that is not so simply resolved.

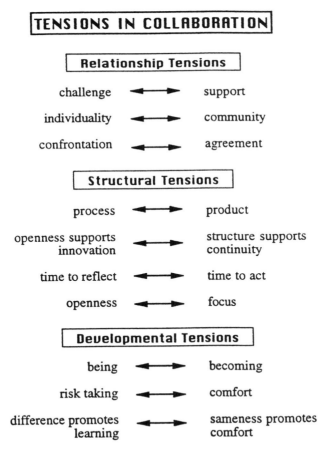

FIGURE 1. Tensions in collaboration.

Maintaining differences in a productive tension is difficult. New participants in our PDS carry cautious assumptions similar to our beginning attitudes. It takes time to rethink differences in ways that welcome rather than avoid them. But even as we try to rethink our assumptions about differences, reality exceeds our categories (Connolly, 1991). Reality is messier than our theoretical categories suggest. Further, we cannot make all differences work in a productive tension, and maybe should not try. Some differences are destructive and do not, cannot, be made productive. How to use this concept of productive tensions while we continue to be critical of both the categories and assumptions is our ongoing challenge.

DIALOGUE

Our third theme is learning through dialogue. Dialogue has become the means by which we examine and learn from our differences. Dialogue for us is a conversation where your convictions are on display for all to see. It is a "growth" environment where you never know exactly what will happen, except that ideas will be shared in a spirit of learning and understandings will develop beyond your individual capacity. Dialogue is a social negotiation of ideas—ideas shared freely, critically, and in ways that nurture rather than destroy. Dialogue is dependent on differences. If we all had the same opinions, or kept our ideas to ourselves, dialogue could not occur. It is because of differences that dialogue is possible, and this promotes our learning. The productivity of tensions is thus sustained through dialogue.

Peter Senge (1990), using work of David Bohm's (1996), makes a distinction between dialogue and the more typical organizational discourse that he calls *discussion*. Discussion is helpful for getting business done. It is goal oriented, and aimed at making decisions. In a discussion, participants argue their positions in order to convince others and have their views accepted by the group. Learning may happen in the process, but the goals are pragmatic. By contrast, the purpose of dialogue "is to go beyond any one individual's understanding. . . . [Participants in a dialogue] gain insights that simply could not be achieved individually" (Senge, p. 241). In a dialogue the goal is learning, not convincing; we offer our ideas to others with the risk that they may be altered in ways we cannot anticipate. These distinctions are not always clear in practice, but they have helped us be more reflective about the kinds of conversations we are having.

Differences of opinion in the group expand the potential of dialogue because they create the tensions that make learning possible. Another important distinction between dialogue and discussion is the interplay between the individual and group associated with dialogue. In dialogue, participants strive to "suspend" roles, assumptions, and judgments. To suspend them is not to ignore or dispense with them; to suspend these elements is to hang them in front of ourselves and the rest of the dialogue participants. We then look at the conversation through these filters in order to recognize and problematize that which mediates our interactions. The result of this kind of dialogue is group learning that occurs from the interaction among individuals; at the same time, growth in self-understanding occurs as individuals use what the group learns as a lens to look inward. We learn as multiple ideas interact, but we also learn as we "recognize" and reflect on things that mediate our experience with the world.

ACADEMIC ASIDE: A DEWEYAN READING OF DIALOGUE

Our interpretation of dialogue needs to be distinguished from more usual forms of dialogue that have linear, rational, and problem solving orientations. Mary Leach (1994/1995), in an article entitled "(Re)searching Dewey for Feminist Imaginaries: Linguistic Continuity, Discourse, and Gossip," uses Dewey to do a feminist reading of various forms of discourse, including "serious gossip." From this reading, she sees the current calls for *dialogue* in educational and national debates as exhibiting:

> the (male) "reflecting mind," which in liberal culture poses as some ideology-free discourse in which gendered, raced, sexed relations, or privilege and power, do not exist. (p. 132)

It is against this type of de-gendered, de-raced, and de-sexed conception of dialogue that we are struggling to reinvent what I would argue is a feminist dialogue. We are trying to interrogate the privilege and power inherent in our conversations and relationships.

For Leach, gossip ("talk that deals with what matters in community affairs") is a form of communicating which, because it stands in contrast to traditional forms of dialogue, "can help us to think otherwise about the prevailing norms" (p. 132). Gossip has a "nomadic quality" that

> can be translated into a feminist problematic in philosophy which helps us address fundamental traits of the patriarchal theoretical system: its chronic denial of recognition to states of flow, fluidity, incompleteness, inconclusiveness, and the relational import of engagement: the *becoming* that emerges in the personal transaction of talking. (p. 132)

Our conversations, which we call dialogues, are closer to Leach's sense of gossip than to rational modes of discourse. We gossip about our community affairs—about a struggling student in our classroom, about a fragile relationship in our school, about feeling inadequate in new PDS roles. These are not topics that lend themselves well to linear, rationalized, problem solving approaches. Rather, we put ourselves at risk in order to share, learn, and rethink ourselves in the middle of a conversation with others. We watch ourselves "becoming" (in Dewey's sense) as we participate in a collaborative community of our own discursive construction.

We are continually frustrated, however, with how hard it is to create places and spaces for the dialogue that supports this kind of learning. We find dialogue is most difficult to do in our large group at Thursday meetings—too many people, not enough time, too many things to talk about. Dialogue for us most often happens in smaller continuous groups, but even here people come and go, and schedules, energy, and personalities get in the way. Smaller dialogue groups, however, are problematic in another sense. There is always the danger that as we get too close and too comfortable with each other we will lose the novelty and the difference upon which dialogue depends.

The sustenance we obtain from learning through dialogue is something we have come to crave, but we also have to be careful about why we crave it and why we want to sustain it. We have to be watchful as well that some differences are not silenced in favor of others. There are times when the differences between schools and universities, because they are obvious aspects of our agenda, are easier to talk about than are the differences reflecting class, gender, and culture. Dialogue, like democracy, is enhanced by continual vigilance into the layers of our differences, not just those at the surface.

Dialogue is often unsettling. Contradictions, insecurities, and ambiguities surface as we challenge each other's thinking. Dialogue stirs up the pot more often than it makes a perfect soup. Questions and challenges make us uneasy. It takes some rethinking to value this state of being, even to yearn after the complexities and contradictions.

Finally we acknowledge that the self-awareness that is required for dialogue can be only partial. While we struggle to be aware of our assumptions and motives, such knowledge is elusive and always incomplete. Finally, if collaboration depends on trusting, respectful relationships, as we will argue throughout this book, then dialogue will require examination of the multiple aspects of our social and professional lives and the moral and ethical issues that are always inherent in them. This goal often exceeds our grasp, although dialogue gets us further into them than is typical in our less collaborative institutional contexts.

CONCLUSION

Dialogue is elusive. Living in tensions is difficult. Yet many of us judge the quality of a meeting and the strength of our collaboration by whether enough dialogue has occurred to make collaborative work and its challenges worthwhile. Elusive as dialogue is, we search for ways to work that encourage it across our differences and in turn promote learning and growth.

While many of us are attracted to these ways of rethinking and talking about differences, we do not want to imply that everyone in our group finds these concepts useful. One of the doctoral students in her first year in the PDS commented:

All this talk about tensions is driving me crazy—tensions, tensions, tensions. Meanwhile, things at my school are falling apart. There must be a better way to talk about what's going on in this PDS.

While there are differences in our group about how best to deal with our differences, the ideas of tensions and dialogue have helped some of us to reconstruct how we think about and work collaboratively.

The Quandary of Parenthood

J. Michael Thomas

Lakoff and Johnson (1980) argue,

"[Metaphor] permits an understanding of one kind of experience in terms of another, creating coherence by virtue of imposing gestalts that are structured by natural dimensions of experience. New metaphors are capable of creating new understandings, and, therefore, new realities." (p. 235)

In this first interlude, Mike Thomas uses the metaphor of an oversized egg to think about the development of a collaborative project.

My metaphor for our PDS is that of a huge egg produced by the uncomfortable, and some say ill-advised, union of a cocky, overcommitted rooster with a frazzled, suspicious, and underappreciated hen. Both parents are surprised at the size of what they have produced and a little frightened of the prospects of what might ultimately emerge from it. These feelings only intensify as they listen to the discordant and often grating noises that emerge from the egg.

As the unlikely pair wait for the egg to hatch, the question that dominates both of their minds is: should we continue to provide the sustenance necessary for this egg to hatch, grow, and develop, knowing full well that we may not be able to support, let alone control, whatever it becomes, or should we simply let it be, to see if it develops the strength, the staying power, and the sense of purpose necessary to make its way in the world?

Neither choice seems very palatable in the moment, and besides, lots of other, more normal eggs are also ready to hatch. But as the two contemplate their next move, they hear the farmer say, "It's too late now. You've already gone and done it."

CHAPTER 2

One Telling of Our History

Marilyn Johnston

This chapter gives a history of the collaborative project from one participant's point of view. In telling this story, I foreshadow the issues, assumptions, and problems that occur throughout the book. Robert Altman directed a movie, *Short Cuts*, in which numerous short vignettes rather unexpectedly come together at the end to make a cohesive story. The history of our PDS does not come together as easily because our collaboration is not a tidy tale. The various aspects and happenings in our project are not as easily tied together as is a film script; rather, we present many stories of unresolved issues, intended as much to disrupt and provoke as to offer what we have learned.

This chapter is my rendering of our history. I make no claims for objectivity, although I try to avoid an egotistical account. I use my experience as co-coordinator, researcher, grant writer, group member, and book writer/editor to construct this interpretive account. I include the attitudes and questions that I brought into the collaborative project in order to explain my influence. While I claim some influence, as you will see, I share the project's direction and character with many others in this book.

Our PDS project went through a number of transformations. The idea began in a seminar I taught on collaborative theories and research (spring 1990); it moved into a funded curricular project related to the 1992 Columbian Quincentenary (January 1991); and then it became a professional development school (spring 1991). This is a circuitous route to becoming a PDS, but themes and people provide continuity of both ideas and purposes.

The conceptual cornerstones of this book—*dealing with differences, the productivity of tensions*, and *learning through dialogue*—weave their way through our development. Learning to deal with differences and tensions as theoretical ideas evolved as we confronted problems in our practices. Dialogue occurred in practice for some time before we found good ways to theorize about it. All three ideas evolved slowly and are interactive. Together they support our general goal to work collaboratively (see chapter 1).

A BRIEF PERSONAL CONTEXT

As an elementary classroom teacher in the 1960s, like many other educators, I moved from traditional instruction to more child-centered approaches. In particular, I became intrigued with developing democratic classrooms. During the last eight years of my classroom teaching experience, I taught in a parent-cooperative child-centered optional instructional program where parents, teachers, and children directed the program together and developed the learning experiences, which included learning for teachers and parents (Rogoff, Turkanis, & Bartlett, in press).

When I moved to a position at the University of Utah, I was involved in some school/university collaborative projects. One was a cooperative master's degree program designed with a local school district to support the interests of the district as well as meet the requirements for graduate-level degrees. I also did some collaborative research with four teachers. These began in rather traditional modes (I was studying the teachers) and moved into more collaborative studies and written reports (Hunsaker & Johnston, 1992; Cryns & Johnston, 1993).

I went to Ohio State University (OSU) in 1988, the year after the college faculty voted to join the Holmes Group, a consortium of research universities with a national agenda to reform teacher education (Holmes Group, 1986, 1990, & 1995). Evidently I missed some rather hearty debates about this choice, but the direction of the college was clear when I arrived. It was moving to post-baccalaureate teacher education and PDSs. I felt generally positive about these developments.

While I had previously been involved in collaborative endeavors, I had not taken time to read much of the literature specific to collaboration or to think through the theoretical problems. I spent my first year at OSU reading in this area and in the spring quarter of my second year offered a graduate seminar. We looked at collaboration between students (examining assumptions and doing research on cooperative learning and democratic classrooms), between teachers (studying teaming and teacher support groups), and between schools and universities (working particularly on collaborative research).

FUNDING AND PLANNING

During the quarter I taught the seminar, the OSU Columbian Quincentenary Committee accepted a proposal of mine to initiate a school/university collaborative project related to the Columbian Quincentenary (an event of high interest in Columbus, Ohio, prior to 1992). Four of the doctoral students in the class and three others were interested in continuing discussions on collaboration and in helping me to design this project. We met weekly throughout the summer to plan it. Combining support from the grant and funded positions to supervise undergraduate certification students, several doctoral students continued with financial support during the fall quarter. We worked on designing the project's research component and continued our discussions of collaboration. Three of the students from this group and I decided during the fall quarter to read some philosophical hermeneutics. We were looking for interpretive frameworks for the research we intended to conduct.

The reading group turned out to be more important than I realized at the time. We had tried to be collaborative and nonhierarchical in our discussion/planning group. I continually raised questions about issues of our relationships and working processes. I also tried to ask questions more than provide answers. This was not particularly difficult because we were struggling with complicated issues, and I frankly did not have ready solutions for many of the problems we faced. Yet I was often positioned as an authority. Several of the students confessed later that they thought I really did know "the answers" but was trying not to impose them.

This situation is understandable. Regardless of how egalitarian I tried to be, I was the adviser for several of the students and sat on dissertation and exam committees where judgments were made in hierarchical ways. It was hard to switch back and forth from egalitarian relationships to hierarchical ones.

Difficulty in this area, as one might expect, varied among the doctoral students and also seemed to correlate to how far each had gone in his or her doctoral studies. The goal of more mutual relationships seemed more challenging for the first-year students than for those who were further along. Of course, there is variation here associated with differences in personalities and backgrounds. (See the section "Rick's Roles" in chapter 4 for one doctoral student's perspective.)

In the reading group we developed a more collaborative relationship than we'd been able to in the discussion/planning group. We were all reading new material. It was clear that I, too, was struggling to interpret these texts. Each week we came with a paragraph we'd written about our reading. They could see me shaping and reshaping my ideas in light of their ideas and our group interpretations. It may be that the collaboration was more easily recognized because we were dealing with academic topics. I did not realize until later that this more obvious struggling together was building trust in the possibility of collaborative work. This, in turn, influenced our work in the larger group.

A READING GROUP

I also joined a group of 10 faculty women from several colleges across campus who were interested in reading post-modern feminist readings. We call ourselves the "PMS group" (Post-Modern Study group). Five years later we still meet regularly. The readings are not easily accessible or directly applicable to my colleagues in the collaborative project, although I've done some directed readings with a couple of the doctoral students. Many of the ideas from these readings, however, have influenced my perspective and purposes.

A post-modern perspective has provided me with another reference point for thinking about collaborative norms (Johnston, 1994). In particular, I have been interested in discussions of language and contextuality, historicity and situatedness, multiple voices and selves, experimental approaches to constructing texts, and the relational and political aspects of research methodologies (see chapter 7). This group has supported my willingness to live on the edge of my own ideas and allowed me to do so more than I ever could have without them. Both my colleagues and the readings have buffeted my natural tendencies to settle into the comfort zone of more traditional positions.

ACADEMIC ASIDE: VIEWING OUR HISTORY

One author we read in my PMS reading group was Walter Benjamin (1968). While he was an exception to the feminist post-modern writers we typically read, Benjamin was provocative in many ways. His writings pushed me to think about positionality in relation to the history of this PDS project. Walter Benjamin uses the image of an angel of history who walks backward into the future. In contrast, Hans Gadamer (1976, 1984) (who we read in the doctoral students' reading group) saw history, and our prejudices and assumptions, behind our backs, thus positioning us with our eyes to the future.

Benjamin owned Paul Klee's painting *Angelus Novus*. The image of the angel is centered on the page and has no background. The angel figure has a startled look on his face. His eyes are staring toward the viewer, his mouth is open, and his wings are spread. Benjamin uses the image of this angel in different ways, including seeing it as a metaphor for history (1968). After describing the visual characteristics of Klee's painting, he writes:

> This is how one pictures the angel of history. His face is turned toward the past. Where we perceive a chain of events, he sees one single catastrophe which keeps piling wreckage upon wreckage and hurls it in front of his feet. The angel would like to stay, awaken the dead, and make whole what has been smashed. But a storm is blowing from Paradise; it has got caught in his wings with such

violence that the angel can no longer close them. This storm irresistibly propels him into the future to which his back is turned, while the pile of debris before him grows skyward. This storm is what we call progress. (pp. 257–258)

Benjamin is writing during the development of Fascism and Nazism moving into World War II. The angel, flying backward into the future vividly captures his Jewish perspective on the world around him and the unknown character of his own destiny. He committed suicide in 1940.

Gadamer, a fellow German writing more than 40 years later (1984), uses a contrasting image of positionality related to history. Gadamer sees history as behind our backs rather than in full view in front of us, as it is for Benjamin's angel. It is behind our backs, because while it influences our thinking and ways of being, it is invisible to us:

History does not belong to us, but we belong to it. Long before we understand ourselves through the process of self-examination, we understand ourselves in a self-evident way in the family, society, and state in which we live. . . . The self-awareness of the individual is only a flickering in the closed circuits of historical life. (p. 245)

We are constituted within a social and historical context long before we can be aware of ourselves as individuals. For Gadamer, this unknowability is explained by our construction within language: "We are always already encompassed by the language that is our own" (Gadamer, 1976, p. 62), and it is part of the nature of language to have "a completely unfathomable unconsciousness of itself" (p. 62). He calls our assumptions and ideas, constituted through language, our "prejudices." They "constitute the initial directedness of our whole ability to experience" (p. 9). Social interactions with texts and with other people help us to become more aware of our prejudices, but this is always partial and ongoing.

These are interesting images to use in relation to collaborative work. If we focus intently, as does the angel, on the piles of debris gathering at our feet, we might see educational systems inadequate to the task of addressing contemporary issues, particularly in urban areas. We might stand in horror at the failure of past attempts to change a system which seems incalcitrant and crumbling beneath the weight of the demands put on it to save a society reeking with crime, violence, and poverty. We might also feel flung into a blind future with wings that will not allow us to fly. Gadamer, on the other hand, makes us cautious about thinking that we can "see" our history, but he gives us a more hopeful future. From this point of view, social interactions with others can help us examine our prejudices and expand our horizons in ways that lead to new understandings.

Collaborative endeavors depend on individuals who are willing to talk across their different horizons and are open to an increased awareness of their own prejudices. In this sense, Gadamer gives us a perspective that faces into a future where dialogue and self-knowledge, however difficult and partial, have the potential to create increased understandings.

ROMANTICIZING COLLABORATION

My reading, teaching, and discussion of collaboration had an interesting consequence. They crystallized a set of arguments for my theoretical assumptions, but they also led to an idealized or romanticized view of how these ideas would work in practice. From this perspective, my previous school/university endeavors seemed only marginally collaborative and still heavily dominated by university control and ideas. Not knowing how to make such efforts more collaborative, I tended to push the requirements of collaboration to their extreme. A couple of things supported this tendency.

First, much of the literature on collaboration at that time (the late 1980s) articulated requirements for collaboration but lacked clear definitions or practical advice. Many pieces described the difficulties, the differences between professors and teachers, and the enormous time requirements. The authors, however, seldom dealt with the complex maneuvering required to develop collaborative relationships or provided careful definitions of concepts like parity and mutuality.

A second influence on my approach to collaboration was a political one. My 10 years of experience in higher education, and more recent readings and discussions, confirmed the critiques I had read in national reports (Carnegie Forum on Education and the Economy, 1986; Holmes Group, 1986, 1990, 1995). I was convinced that teacher education was in trouble. I was eager to try something different. I embraced collaboration as a way to create change. With both idealized views and an acute sensitivity to issues related to the hierarchies between school and university, we moved toward inviting schools into the project.

RECRUITING THE SCHOOL GROUPS

By winter quarter of the next year, we had six schools ready to work with us on the Quincentenary project. As I talked to schools about participating, I described the social studies focus of the Columbian Quincentenary. This part was fairly straightforward and clear. We would study the issues related to the cultural encounters resulting from Christopher Columbus's trips to the Americas and then design model projects in the schools that would be open to visitors during 1992. The city of Columbus anticipated a large influx of tourists that year. The OSU Columbian Quincentenary Committee that funded the collaborative project and the city Quincentenary Committee were both excited about having the model school projects on display. As a social studies faculty member, I saw the controversies surrounding the "Celebrations" (as the city logo described them) as ripe territory for issues of multiculturalism, interpretations of history, and the role of social studies in the curriculum.

I also talked about the intended collaborative nature of the project. This part of the project was necessarily vague and generally uninteresting to the teachers. I said that we would make collaborative decisions in the group and each school group would make its own decisions about its individual school Quincentenary project. I could not tell at the time whether they did not trust what I was saying or whether they were indifferent to the topic. At the end of my description, I mentioned the possibility of graduate credit; this drew considerable interest.

The idea of a citywide model school project required participation of several schools in different parts of the city. We chose schools for this project to include urban, suburban, and parochial schools, alternative and traditional instructional programs, and student populations with a wide range of cultural and socioeconomic differences. This diversity also supported my interest in multicultural issues and work with urban schools. The doctoral students and I had decided ahead of time that at least five teachers and the principal from a school had to commit to the weekly meetings to join the Quincentenary project. We argued that a critical mass of participants from a school was necessary to building a school Quincentenary project and that we needed to talk on a regular basis if we were going to be collaborative.

BEGINNING WITH THE SCHOOLS

We had our first meeting in one school during the first week of winter quarter 1991. There were some 45 people present. After the schools' representatives introduced themselves, a couple of the doctoral students and I went over basic information, much as we had done in the individual meetings with the invited schools. We emphasized again the collaborative goals of the Quincentenary project and said we had many decisions to make in order to get our project under way. We identified some of the decision making topics and began discussions on a few of them. At the end there were questions about registering for credit, and we decided where to meet the next week. After so much planning and anticipation, this first meeting felt disappointing. There'd been little interaction and university participants had done most of the talking.

There were a number of striking aspects of our first-quarter meetings. First, we had not anticipated how unusual it was for teachers to meet in an ongoing way with their counterparts from other schools and districts. Teachers often go to meetings and inservice presentations with teachers outside their buildings, but to work on a regular basis with teachers from such varied settings was different and difficult. Each Thursday night we spent time making decisions and then either heard from a speaker related to the Quincentenary or did planning in school groups. After several weeks of plodding through decisions about how we would be organized, questions about the value of this decision making emerged. Many teachers preferred to spend more time on their school projects. There were also questions (that were less publicly addressed) about the value of urban and suburban schools working together.

The Quincentenary projects that were emerging were varied. One school decided to develop a landscaped area outdoors that would be called the Discovery Garden. It would provide an on-site laboratory to do science, create art projects, and study social and environmental issues. An integrated curriculum was planned. Parents and local business people were solicited to help with this rather extensive endeavor. Another school was developing the theme of voyages through the Americas looking at cultural encounters in North and South America with a focus on multicultural education. Different grade levels studied different countries, and the school held a cultural fair as a culminating event.

The wide variation and scope of the Quincentenary projects made it difficult to see the value of sharing across schools. Teachers preferred to work in their own school groups. Also, as projects began to take shape, a competitive edge was developing between schools to create bigger and better projects. (See chapters 8 and 9 for case studies of the beginnings of collaboration at two schools.)

My role was also problematic during the first quarter. I tried in as many ways as possible to de-position myself as the director of the project. I continually asked for suggestions, refused to define the outline of the project (except for the collaborative nature of the process), and tried to put other people in front of the group as much as possible. Many of the teachers had signed up for university credit and expected a syllabus. Many times in this book you will see mention of their initial frustrations. (In particular, see the case studies in chapters 8 and 9.)

In retrospect, I think I overdid the attempt to position myself in nonhierarchical ways. It probably caused more frustration than was necessary, though it clearly made a point. It kept my role and the issues of hierarchical relationships between schools and universities as a major topic of discussion, but it obviated a more productive interaction between them. My refusal to be directive meant that the university voice was absent from some of the conversations, deliberately silenced in favor of the teachers' perspective. From a theoretical point of view, I withheld one pole of the tension that could have supported teachers' learning as well as mine.

ACADEMIC ASIDE: DECONSTRUCTION AND COLLABORATION

Putting my position up for questioning could be described as an attempt to deconstruct traditional institutional roles. While I did not use this terminology in the group, my goal was to question/deconstruct the power relations between schools and universities and to try and de-position myself from a role that is typically the power position.

Deconstruction has its roots in a long history of critical thinking evident in philosophy since Plato, carrying through to the critical theorists and Marxian scholars of more contemporary times. To critique the unspoken claims behind educational programs and practices (Apple, 1986; Cherryholmes, 1988), to look at what is behind one's back (Gadamer, 1984), to seek possibilities not yet imagined (Greene, 1988), is to ask questions about how things are typically done and how they might be otherwise. Deconstruction adds its own particular flavor to this set of varied strategies. Like other strategies, it has proponents of several colors, and they do not all agree.

What I find provocative in deconstruction is what Judith Butler calls "reusage or redeployment" (1992). She focuses on deconstructing the concept of the self, but the same approach is more generally useful. "To deconstruct is not to negate or dismiss, but to call into question, and, perhaps most important, to open up a term like the subject to a reusage or redeployment that has previously not been authorized" (p. 15).

Deconstruction pushes beyond imagining new possibilities to questioning the political context within which existing practices reside. Why is it that we continue to work in ways that are antithetical to collaboration? Why are institutions organized this way, and what are the effects on those of us who live within them? From this perspective, we are reminded that deconstruction and redeployment will be a political act that will bump up against what has been authorized. We are further reminded that power structures pervade our work and that by deconstructing and making apparent these often unseen and unspoken forces, we expose and threaten the very structures that undergird the working relations within which we still reside.

As we deconstruct, we work within as we try to change. This is somewhat analogous to tearing down a building while trying to build a new one. A deconstruction is typically more than remodeling. It requires a critical reassessment of the values and principles that adhere in the politics and power of present relations.

Of course, I could not de-position myself entirely. I often led the decision-making sessions. I represented the university point of view when information or perspectives were needed. I was also deeply committed to the success of the project and was not ready to let things fall apart. I played a leadership role even as I tried not to. Many of our initial papers and conference presentations deal with topics of role and hierarchy (see appendix A). The question of my role and actions set in motion a particular set of attitudes toward collaboration that have continued to influence our subsequent work together (see the section "Marilyn's Roles" in chapter 4).

In subsequent years the topics of hierarchy and authority have not been discussed much. A more secure sense of continuity and history, some established traditions, and increased teacher assertiveness make these less critical topics. As the co-coordinating team has enlarged and new people have come into the PDS, other concerns have taken center stage. Mike Thomas (a clinical educator and co-coordinator) has engendered a lot of interest in systems theories, and we have found Roland Barth (on organizations that support adult learning, 1990) and Peter Senge (on "learning organizations," 1990) useful in evaluating how our organizational structure promotes learning, dialogue, and collegiality. Interest in action research has spread to the whole group and Thursday nights are largely spent in Project Groups, sharing ideas and readings and developing inquiry projects. The energy and learning developing in these smaller groups are in tension with the larger issues that connect us as a group. As we spend less time as a whole group, we lose a sense of this connectedness, yet we profit from the dialogue which more often happens in these smaller groups.

ROLE OF THE DOCTORAL STUDENTS

The initial seminar and subsequent discussions with the doctoral students were my "think tank" preparation for the overall project. We read and talked a lot about collaboration. As we started with the school groups in January 1991, a number of doctoral students continued to meet weekly. We discussed what was going on and made plans for the next weekly meeting. The issues were as intriguing after we started the Quincentenary project as they'd been before.

A major topic of discussion in our weekly meetings was the doctoral student's role in the schools. By the fall quarter of 1991, there were enough doctoral students supported within the project to have one in each school.

(At this point we began to call them graduate associates, or GAs, because most were receiving support from the department to "supervise student teachers.") The challenge was to create a collaborative role for them. In a traditional supervisory role, the university supervisor seldom got to know the cooperating teachers well and was usually working with students in several schools. In our case, they were assigned to a school for the year. We decided that they should individually work out their roles collaboratively with the teachers and student teachers in their schools. Rather than taking a traditional supervising role, they searched for ways to integrate themselves into the life of the school as they worked with teachers and student teachers.

We intended to have a lot of flexibility, and consequently there was a need for much conversation and negotiation. This worked well in some cases and less well in others. As new teachers and doctoral students came into the project in subsequent years, figuring out how to negotiate their roles and responsibilities prompted many good conversations, much individual initiative and growth, and a fair amount of frustration.

As with our idealization of collaboration in general, we initially idealized the role of the GAs. Integrating oneself into the life of the school was difficult to do as a non-staff person who was on site only 10 to 15 hours a week. There were traditional expectations for university supervisors that needed to be overcome, and there was never enough time (see the section "Rick's Roles" in chapter 4). Over the years we have moderated this talk about self-defined roles and integrating into the school life, although there is still variation in how doctoral students work in their schools.

While the challenges have been many, the GAs have been a very important part of this project. They have been the primary university link in the schools. Many, especially those who have been with the project for more than a year (average tenure is two years; the range is one to four years), established strong relationships with teachers, worked on initiatives in the schools, helped to write grants, collaborated on action research, substitute taught (in emergency situations), did demonstration teaching, and worked closely with the interns. Many have also co-taught methods courses.

PDS PROPOSAL

By the middle of spring quarter 1991, most of the schools had designed the focus of their Quincentenary projects and were excited about developing their school-based activities. At this time the college issued a call for proposals for professional development schools. The request for proposals (RFP) required demonstration of collaboration between a school or schools and a university faculty. Because we were already working collaboratively in our Quincentenary project and because I had placed my undergraduate student teachers in our schools, we met the requirements.

I was very interested in the possibility of our schools becoming a PDS, but I had not anticipated that proposals would be required on such a short time line. There was not enough time to make an informed decision, and many did not understand the concept of a PDS or the direction of the college. Committees representing school districts, teacher associations, school boards, and university faculty had been meeting for six months to set up the organization within the college and with the school districts. The dean subsequently set up meetings in school districts that some of our participants attended, but the concept of a PDS was still vague to most. We talked about the possibility of submitting a proposal in a Thursday meeting, held a couple of open after-school meetings to discuss it further, and submitted a proposal.

Our hastily written proposal was accepted in May. Our proposal focused on four of the Holmes Group goals that most closely fit our current work—teacher education reform, professional development, inquiry, and urban education issues. As we were the only PDS associated with the Elementary and Early Childhood Program, we were quickly offered the opportunity to work with the newly established MEd cohort of students who had just been admitted and would start their courses in June. Many of the teachers were interested in having student teachers, so we agreed to take the MEd students. It didn't take us long to realize that we were compounding our purposes and had assumed a very heavy agenda for our second year.

PLANNING FOR THE MEd STUDENTS

We scheduled a week in June, shortly after school was out, to deal with the planning necessary to work with the MEd students. I couched the PDS agenda in terms of teachers and faculty working together to solve some of the problems of teacher education. The teachers readily agreed that there were problems.

As we began our week-long planning session, I kept pushing to do things differently. How could we set up schedules, courses, and experiences to solve problems with school placements in the traditional model? How could we make better connections between methods courses and field placements—between theory and practice? What kinds of things should the field experience provide for MEd students? How could university participants be more connected to schools and school participants more connected to the university?

Most of the teachers had never been asked to shape a university program. Some were hesitant to make suggestions; others were eager to fix problems they had experienced with previous student teachers. There were courses prescribed by the newly approved MEd certification program, but outside of the course titles there was a lot of wiggle room. The university faculties who were assigned to teach the MEd courses met with us for one morning session, but most of the decisions about schedules and field requirements were defined by the teachers.

The faculty teaching the methods courses were not particularly interested in collaborative planning, but they were endlessly willing to adjust to the schedules designed by the teachers. Most were also willing to adjust assignments in light of the teachers' suggestions. The methods instructors (faculty and co-teachers) met every other week to talk about integration across the courses and problems with the students.

Co-Teaching the Methods Courses

Four of the faculty and I agreed to have classroom teachers co-teach our methods courses. I was teaching the MEd social studies methods course and I had two GAs and one classroom teacher (CT) who co-taught the course with me fall and winter quarter (Hohenbrink, 1993; Hohenbrink, Johnston, & Westhoven, 1992, in press). We also had GAs and/or CTs in the language arts, science, and children's literature courses. In subsequent years, many of the courses have been co-taught. This includes one quarter when the dean of the college, Nancy Zimpher, co-taught the pedagogy course with one of our PDS principals; the next year she taught the course to the MEd students and the PDS group on Thursday nights for a quarter.

There were several reasons for co-teaching the courses. Cooperating teachers have historically been critical about "what happens at the university" and have considered university faculty to be out of touch with the real world of schooling. These same complaints are echoed by students. Initially, I figured that if the teachers knew more about the courses, they would have more positive attitudes. Also, I thought it would be an opportunity for them to be exposed to new ideas and strategies that the MEd students were learning. I was sure that they would also bring useful classroom examples into the courses, but I thought co-teaching would primarily "bring the teachers up to date," rather than change the courses much.

In addition to these elitist attitudes, I was anxious to try the co-teaching because I also thought that it would further our collaboration. Just as I intended to spend more time in the schools, I thought teachers spending time at the university was an equally justifiable expectation. Little did I know then how profoundly this co-teaching would influence my purposes and orientation to my social studies methods course as well as the teaching practices of my co-teachers (Hohenbrink, Johnston, & Westhoven, in press; Hohenbrink, 1993).

For example, I came to see the limited usefulness of the decontextualized activities that I used in my classes in contrast to the embedded examples that co-teachers brought from their classrooms. Preservice students were exposed to teachers' thinking about social studies activities within the complexity of their classrooms, and they seemed subsequently more willing to struggle with the problems and variations in their field-based experiences as they tried things in social studies.

I have also come to value the conversations with my co-teachers that led to a curriculum that more clearly represents the pressures and realities of classrooms. As a university professor, I find it is easy to forget how the pressures of competency tests, principal evaluations, and peer pressure influence teacher decision making and teaching. I have not given up my own commitments to social studies as I believe it should ideally be done. Through collaboration, my co-teachers and I can better connect theory and practice and give our students a more well-rounded and realistic look at the challenges and possibilities of teaching social studies.

When I first suggested the idea of co-teaching, few teachers were interested. Although each would be given a substitute for one day a week for two quarters, leaving the classrooms on a regular basis was not an attractive offer. It took one-on-one conversations to convince a few teachers to try it the first year. There were, in practice, many problems for co-teachers, including extra planning for subs, problems with children while they were gone, and, probably most difficult, disapproval from some of their peers. If a consistent sub could be arranged for each week so that there was consistency in instruction, it was much easier on teachers and their students. Over time this has been one of the most important variables in whether teachers felt good about their co-teaching experiences.

They also had some problems working with their university counterparts. Some professors used co-teachers primarily to add related practical examples to their regular lectures. In these situations, teachers often felt that they were not contributing enough to justify time away from their classroom. In other cases, particularly when co-teaching teams stayed together more than a year, there was a good deal of collaborative planning, teaching, and evaluation.

While co-teaching requires a lot of discussion to make practical decisions about the courses, it has also provoked dialogue. The differences between school-based and university perspectives have been the ground to support a great deal of learning and empathy for each other's perspectives and challenges. The idea of learning from our differences is a major theme throughout the book.

Dealing With Multiple Goals

We spent four days of the first year's planning week dealing with organizational issues related to the MEd students (interns) and one day working on our Quincentenary projects. Some teachers were frustrated with the heavy planning required to prepare for the MEd interns because it interfered with their planning for their Quincentenary projects; others were excited about the teacher education aspects. We decided to overlap the two as much as possible. The interns would work with their teachers on the school's Quincentenary project, and their method course assignments, especially in social studies, would be integrated as much as possible. The professional development goal (one of the Holmes Group goals for PDSs) was discussed briefly, but it was set aside until later. The immediate needs of dealing with 24 MEd students took precedence over more personal professional goals. Professional development, we reasoned, would come later, when there was more time.

We were slow to recognize the complementarity of professional development and teacher education. Before the PDS, teachers considered taking student teachers as primarily helping the university do its job. Student teachers were in and out of their classrooms within 10 weeks, and unless there were problems, they caused little disruption to classroom routines.

The new structure of the PDS meant working with interns differently, especially after the first year, when we decided on year-long placements. Long-term intern placements and the collegial relationships that developed between interns and cooperating teachers had a substantial impact on many classrooms. There was more reflection and experimentation in classrooms. There were conversations on Thursday nights. Many questions had to be addressed as we planned and delivered a certification program. What should students get out of field experiences? What do future teachers need to learn? What kind of teachers do we want them to be? These questions were about the program, but they pushed at the edges of our own development as well. The discussions exposed our individual beliefs and interests; we talked explicitly about our ideals and aspirations for the profession. Professional development occurred as we focused on teacher education in spite of our assumptions about their separateness.

We also had a student cohort that promoted our professional development. This again we did not anticipate. Our students, in contrast to many undergraduate students, were generally older and seriously committed to becoming teachers. Many had left high-paying jobs to spend a year in graduate school. Many had families who were making financial sacrifices to support this choice. These were not placid students; they were mature and demanding. They expected a high-quality professional program. In courses and classrooms they asked hard questions. A former computer analyst wondered why the computers were not being used in the classroom. A former stockbroker questioned why math lessons were not made relevant to real-life situations. A sales manager suggested new possibilities for managing a classroom. Many of the teachers and faculty liked and profited from these challenges; others found students arrogant and pushy, and chose in subsequent years to return to work with undergraduate students.

One of the teachers at Second Avenue, Mary Christenson, wrote about the influence of questioning on professional development:

> As teachers at Second Avenue, we first became involved in the Quincentenary project because we thought it would give us ways to improve the school and everyone else. Then we became a PDS and along came the interns and all the questions they were asking us about our teaching. We were suddenly forced to look at and defend our own practices. The result of all this questioning has been a lot of personal and professional growth. Personally, I have tried many new things in my teaching and am presently doing an action research study of cooperative learning groups in my urban class-room. (March 1996)

In subsequent years, we developed more focused plans for professional development to provide more systematic learning opportunities. In the third year, we organized interest groups—small groups of teachers who studied a particular topic. About half the teachers participated. They were granted one day a month release time by their school districts to study together and do school visits. Teachers have also designed and conducted action research, presented at national conferences, and written for publication. The richness of these experiences led to the development of Project Groups at Thursday meetings, which means that inquiry, once the province of a small and separate group, now permeates everything we do. All of these activities have supported professional development and extend beyond the typical roles of teachers and cooperating teachers.

THE STEERING COMMITTEE

In the second year we decided to have a steering committee. It would have a representative from each school, a GA representative, and me (I was the only university faculty member participating at this time). The steering committee would plan the Thursday night meetings and deal with issues that did not need to go to the whole group.

The committee was set up in response to ongoing frustrations over how much time we spent making decisions on Thursday nights. Sometimes there were so many housekeeping tasks (where to meet, who would create the agendas, how to handle snacks, etc.) that we had little time left for the big issues. At this time we had few precedents to rely on when making practical decisions. It was a convincing argument that some of these decisions could be made more efficiently by a smaller group.

Part of this decision to have a steering committee was fueled by a lack of assertiveness in the larger group. One of the teachers, Geri Granger, recently recounted a vivid memory she had of one such discussion.

> The Thursday meeting was at my school, so I invited several of the teachers in my building to go to the meeting. I was trying to recruit more teachers into the PDS. We got into this discussion of whether we should have the supervision forms on different colors of paper, indicating the forms required for each quarter. For whatever reason, there was this endless discussion about whether the forms should be red and gray, vanilla and green, or fluorescent. Then we discussed the format to be used and whether the interns or the cooperating teacher should keep the forms. My teacher colleagues, one by one, excused themselves as the discussion proceeded. No one, including me, felt comfortable enough to say, "This is stupid, let's go on to something important."

Such frustrating discussions, as well as the sheer number of issues to be discussed, led to the decision to have a steering committee.

It began meeting on Wednesdays, after school. The first few meetings were a bit shaky, but then we began having very interesting discussions. As we tried to make practical decisions, issues about collaborative norms and purposes were always apparent. Our scheduled hour-and-a-half meetings often ran long. Sometimes we didn't get decisions made because we went off on an interesting tangent. We tried to take some of these conversations back to the group, but our attempts were seldom successful. Somehow, we couldn't replicate the intriguing discussions of the steering committee in the larger group. Even when we broke into small groups, it was hard to get discussions going.

By the end of the year, dissatisfaction with the steering committee was raised in the larger group. After some discussion, the steering committee was disbanded. The dissatisfaction was not with the kinds of decisions the steering committee was making, but rather with the way their decision making limited collaboration in the larger group. Steering committee members were feeling enthusiastic and collaborative. Those who weren't on the committee felt left out of the loop. The research group came to call this situation, which occurred in other contexts, the "in-group/out-group" problem. Disbanding the steering committee meant that we were back to discussing everything in the group.

We did, however, get better at discussions. Mary Christenson took a year off from the PDS. She wrote about her impressions when she came back to the group a year later.

It happened at approximately 9:30 on a warm June morning, one day after the school year had ended. Suddenly I experienced a strange unsettling feeling that I had done all this before. I look around. Was this simply déjà vu, or was it something else? Even though it had been a year since I had actively participated in PDS, I was certain that I had been in this room, with these people, discussing the exact same issues 12 months earlier.

At first I was amused. Perhaps I had crossed back over some strange wrinkle in time, and it was actually early summer of 1992, not 1993. Then I became concerned. Did this mean that we had made no progress toward resolving our larger issues in the year I was gone?

As I listened to the conversations, I realized the major difference a year had made. Although issues like scheduling and how to deal with co-teaching were being discussed again, there was a new level of experience in the room to bring to the conversation. This is what successful change is all about: people who care about improving education take risks and try new things. Then they take what they have learned and are willing to change once again. (March 1995)

Change takes time but the effects are cumulative over time as we have slowly learned how to talk to each other differently and take risks in a supportive collegial group.

AGENDAS AND COMMUNICATION

I do not want to leave the impression that our weekly meetings have been totally open and unstructured. While there has been much flexibility, we have used a variety of strategies to set agendas and to get them out ahead of time.

E-mail communication was particularly helpful in this regard. During the second year the college provided a computer and modem for each school and a graduate student to help us set up and learn how to do E-mail. The challenges, both technological and personnel, could fill a book, but eventually we could communicate regularly between schools and the university. Minutes of each week's meeting and plans for the next week are now regularly on E-mail. One person in each school checks the E-mail regularly and gets copies out to others.

If a teacher is taking credit or has an intern placed in his or her room, he or she must attend Thursday meetings regularly. Other teachers are welcome at any time. In some schools, all or most teachers have been involved in PDS at some time. This has helped with communication between PDS and non-

PDS teachers, as well as allowing the PDS to take advantage of the expertise of many teachers, some of whom cannot attend regularly because of other commitments.

Decision Making Struggles

Some of the difficulty associated with decision making was related to teacher assertiveness. Especially in the beginning, it felt like pulling teeth to get decisions made. It was difficult to get school participants to speak up. After meetings were over, I received reports that people had been unhappy with this or that, but they would not speak up *while the issue was being discussed*. There were probably several reasons for this. For one, many of the teachers wanted me to make the decisions. It seemed more efficient, safer, and typical of how schools and universities usually work together. We had not had time to build trust, many were confused by both my rhetoric and my actions, and most had not been in educational groups where dissension was valued. We have come to appreciate the striking differences between schools and universities with respect to asserting disagreements. Many teachers feel that their schools are not safe places to disagree. If you object to something or disagree with a colleague, you are considered uncooperative or aggressive. At the university, it is expected that you will offer your ideas and heartily debate issues. Professors, much more than teachers, are rewarded for idiosyncratic ideas, and personal opinions are expected. My expectations for fuller teacher involvement were outside the limits of what felt safe for them.

It has taken considerable time for some teachers to feel safe expressing their ideas in the large group; it has been easier in smaller, continuous groups like the steering committee and the research group. For many teachers, having a place to talk outside their school context and to compare notes across schools has created a safe space to examine teaching and political issues that are rarely discussed openly in their schools.

Time: Always an Issue

There never seemed to be enough time. Decision making during our first year with the MEd interns consumed most of our Thursday meetings. The teachers wanted time to work on their Quincentenary projects, but we spent most of our time making decisions about teacher education issues. For the next year, we agreed to what were affectionately, or maybe not so affectionately, called "marathon Thursdays." We divided the evening into segments so we could set time limits. We had a segment for community business, then an hour for Quincentenary project planning, and the last hour for MEd issues and supervision problems. The research group then met for an hour afterward. The meetings started at 4:15 and the research group finished at 8 P.M. Smaller groups sometimes went out for dinner, drinks, or coffee after we'd finished. These were exhausting meetings, but we were accomplishing a great deal and setting up many organizational aspects that have lasted over time.

In subsequent years we could not sustain this time commitment. As our Quincentenary projects were completed during the 1992–1993 school year, we were relieved of one major agenda. As we made decisions about how to do things, our community business agendas were shorter. Of course, there are always issues; things come up. We still schedule time most Thursdays to deal with issues and community business.

A Nagging Issue

One constant problem has been how to decide when a decision is final. After much discussion, we decided not to vote on issues because voting alienated people who disagreed. Our goal was to incorporate and use our differences rather than let them separate us further. So we often talked about things longer than was necessary, or we made a decision and then someone raised a question about it later. Sometimes, going over an issue again felt like progress because there were new issues. At other times, it felt pointless. It was difficult, however, to tell ahead of time which would be productive and who should stop the discussion when it wasn't. As participants have become more assertive, we are dealing more easily with these issues. We also made some policy decisions that helped.

For example, we have a clear policy that our summer planning is time for making the big decisions, scheduling the next year, setting new goals, and making major changes. If you do not attend, you lose your voice in the decision. It was rather painful, coming to this decision, but the need for it was apparent after what we subsequently called our "meeting from hell." During our second summer planning week, we made many decisions to change things. At our first meeting in the fall, we reported back to the whole group. In addition to new teachers from existing schools, we also had a new school joining us. New participants and those not at the summer planning meeting had many questions about new decisions. We spent the whole meeting rehashing what had already been decided. Some of the new teachers never came back. Every single person left feeling frustrated.

Not long after that, we decided that whatever is agreed to during summer planning meetings is final. This decision has stuck firmly and has helped to avoid the rehashing of major decisions.

CLINICAL EDUCATORS/CO-COORDINATORS

One consistent aspect of our PDS has been the wealth of opportunities provided for all of us to assume new roles and responsibilities. These roles have often unexpectedly created situations that have produced much growth and learning. One of the most powerful role change opportunities has been the role of clinical educator (CE). Our first such position was offered when we became a PDS. Each PDS was granted one half-time CE to be a co-coordinator with a university person. Lisa Westhoven, a third-grade teacher in one of our schools, was selected for our PDS. Lisa and I have been the co-coordinators. We facilitate communication and take care of bureaucratic matters. We also meet each month with co-coordinator teams from the other Ohio State PDSs.

At the end of the second year, we were granted a second half-time CE, defined as our PDS ethnographer. Mike Thomas, a teacher from a non- PDS school who had a PhD and research interests that matched our needs, was selected. Mike joined the co-coordinating team the following year, when he became a full-time clinical educator and took over many of my responsibilities as I became a co-coordinator for all the college's PDSs. This year, while I am on sabbatical, Jerry Zutell, another faculty person, has joined the co-coordinating team.

During the third year, outside funding provided support for a new CE role. Teachers in these CE roles were released one day a week to support PDS goals within their school. There were three teachers in three of the schools that were interested. Like other developing aspects of the PDS, these roles were experimental and open ended. These CEs were to promote collaboration, support inquiry, and work with the interns in their building. How to accomplish these goals was left up to each CE. Every CE works closely with the GA in his or her building. They jointly conduct weekly focus group meetings with their MEd interns. They talk about problems that the interns have in their teaching or university courses. Other initiatives are left up to them.

Teachers have had mixed feelings about being released from their teaching responsibilities to co-teach courses at the university or to be clinical educators. Their major hesitancy initially was about leaving their children. Other teachers in their schools also questioned whether they should be leaving their classrooms. It has taken considerable time and experience to alter the assumption that teachers should be individually responsible for their students.

New roles for teachers have affected their relationships with colleagues, raised unsettling questions about the purposes of schooling, and prompted growth at the same time they have caused anxiety and frustrations. Building new institutional roles is not an easy road.

As these roles developed, it seemed natural for the CEs to join the GAs in their weekly meeting. This turned out to be a wonderful idea. It gave the CEs a place to share experiences and problems with their GA partners and to get support for the problems they were facing. The CEs also came to fully participate in the more issues-oriented discussions related to collaboration and reform that had been an ongoing part of the GA meetings.

An interesting phenomenon has occurred this last year. All of the CEs continued from the previous year, but four of the six GAs were new. Toward the end of the year, there were some interesting discussions about the role of the GAs in the PDS, and more particularly, in the GA/CE weekly meetings. Some of them wanted to have a separate meeting because they felt that their issues were not being addressed. The power and influence had shifted to the CEs, and the GAs felt like work hands who performed important supervision duties but had little real voice. Also, many of the GAs had classes on Thursday evenings and missed developing connections to the Project Groups and other things going on in the larger group. The GA/CE meetings had less dialogue occurring because the commitment and trust in the group were not strong enough to support the necessary risk taking. It has taken some difficult talking about these issues to reestablish a context conducive to dialogue. The tensions lost their productive edge as power relations and unattended relationships made the differences feel conflictual rather than supportive of learning.

COLLABORATION OR IMPOSITION?

The doctoral students and I originally agreed to a collaborative approach prior to working with our school colleagues. We were aware of the irony of *imposing* collaborative norms. The school participants had no voice in this decision, and although they joined knowing of this aspect, many would have opted for a more directed approach. Some teachers and schools left because they did not like the ambiguity and time involved in making collaboration decisions. The school Quincentenary projects helped to create a sense of direction and progress but did not solve all the problems.

There were ongoing discussions about these issues. Couldn't we be more efficient and meet less often? Did we really need to talk about every issue as a group? For three years we debated the issue of weekly meetings. A recurring decision to continue weekly meetings was influenced by a few strong voices. Mine was one of them. I was more and more convinced that it took this kind of time to build trusting relationships and shared norms. If we were going to do things differently and make these decisions collaboratively, I was sure it would take time. It is one of the few issues where I feel heavy-handed about my influence. I feared a return to a "university-run" project without the ongoing group conversation.

By the end of the third year, there were only occasional questions about weekly meetings. Their value in terms of professional development and the interactions across schools was positive enough to keep us coming back. It may also have been that people who were not profiting from the weekly meetings left—a kind of self-selection of those in favor of weekly meetings and this form of collaboration.

THE RESEARCH GROUP

The idea and methods of research were also imposed. We did not discuss with the teachers whether we should do the initial research project; rather, we justified it as one of the requirements of the funding. Of course, I had written the proposal with questions that fit my personal research agenda. I probably could have gotten the grant with a much briefer evaluation component. I felt some pressure, however, to do research and publish from work that was going to be time-consuming. I also wanted support for doctoral students and possibilities for dissertations and publishing for them as well.

The plan for the research was to do case studies of the various schools and to ask the question "How is collaboration unfolding differently in each school context?" I was personally interested in the situated nature of the cases and in how collaborative relations, both within schools and between school-based and university-based participants, would be influenced by personalities, school contexts, and institutional constraints. Rick Kerper, one of the doctoral students, agreed to manage the research as part of his assistantship. I was pleased because I saw this as another way to de-position myself from a leadership position. There were unexpected consequences, however, for him. The year before, as a teacher leader in his elementary school position, he had been a *school* person, not a *university* person, and he expected to be thought of as a colleague. Instead, teachers treated him cautiously, as a university person (see the section "Rick's Roles" in chapter 4).

During the first few Thursday meetings, Rick explained the research. We wanted one or two teachers from each school, we would meet for an hour after the regular Thursday meeting, and they could get research course credit. Course credit was the biggest drawing card and we quickly had at least one teacher from each school. As we started, the group included Rick, seven teachers, three GAs, and myself.

The research group agenda was very open ended. We wanted to talk about the issues that teachers found interesting or problematic. The tape recorder was on, as it was for all our PDS meetings. We explained this as an effort to document what we were accomplishing.

Rick's approach to leading the research group had been influenced by our prior discussions on collaboration. He started each meeting with the question, "What shall we talk about tonight?" In the beginning, this was awkward. The teachers did not consider themselves researchers and felt they needed to be taught how to do "real" research. They were puzzled by inquiry that was mostly talking about the meaning of collaboration and what was happening in their schools.

It didn't take long, however, for lively discussions to develop. We often ran over our scheduled time, and many conversations were continued in the parking lot afterward. The similarities and differences between schools were intriguing. It was fascinating to speculate why certain problems appeared in some schools and not in others.

We also had some "data" to discuss. We had asked (or rather, required) that any teacher taking credit write a weekly journal entry and turn it into his or her school "researcher." We read these each week and tried to make sense of the feelings of the larger group. Sometimes we cumulated the responses and fed them back to the school groups or to the larger group for discussion. We began to talk about the tapes of the meetings and journal entries as data and discussed how to use qualitative methodologies to think about them. Grant funds provided substitutes so we could attend an all-day meeting once a quarter. We discussed readings on qualitative research and started to build a conceptual background for thinking about research from this perspective.

The research group, while it was an imposition in the beginning, quickly developed into a forum for hearty conversations about the teachers' concerns. The GAs and I were also often involved in the problems teachers were discussing. Sometimes the topic was our university roles and the ways in which we were supporting or hindering collaboration. One issue that came up frequently was my role. Many times I raised the issue. When I felt guilty about controlling a weekly meeting or wondered how my comments were being perceived, the research group was a context for reflection and feedback. At other times, teachers raised the power issues. My co-coordinator, Lisa Westhoven, took on the self-appointed title "watchdog of hierarchy" and took to calling me and others when she thought there was hierarchical domination. This was done in good humor, but it helped to keep attention on issues of power, role, imposition, and trust. Lisa and I spent many hours together as co-coordinators, and we also co-taught the social studies methods course. We had developed a sense of trust that allowed her to speak up when other teachers might have been hesitant. She modeled a kind of assertive behavior for other teachers.

Some of the issues we talked about in the research group were sensitive and difficult to talk about. For example, some teachers were critical of the collaborative focus and caused dissension within school groups; sometimes principals were not supportive of PDS goals and activities; some teacher researchers felt ostracized in their schools because of their membership in the research group; PDS teachers in some schools felt disapproval from the non-PDS teachers in their buildings. The cross-school nature of the group meant that problems in one school were discussed by people at other schools. This "telling stories out of school" is something teachers rarely do, and this might easily have become a problem. There were, however, no instances I knew of where comments from the research group were carried outside the group in ways that caused problems. A strong sense of trust and mutuality developed in this group, something more than was possible with the large numbers at Thursday meetings.

IN-GROUP/OUT-GROUP

The closeness and trust that developed within the research group were causing problems in the larger group by the end of the first year. The research group was developing a shared sense of collaborative norms, and they contributed disproportionately to large group discussions. They were, therefore, perceived by some as pushy or arrogant. The large group participants also knew that their journal responses were being read by the research group, and some felt that they were being used as guinea pigs for someone else's research purposes.

This situation, what came to be called the "in-group/out-group" problem, was much discussed by the research group. We decided to address the issue directly in the summer planning meeting in June. During the week, we conducted a research group session with the rest of the group observing. We chose an interesting (but nonsensitive) current issue and talked in our usual way. Rick started by asking, "What shall we talk about?" Someone described the problem and we were off. After about thirty minutes of a typically interesting discussion, we opened it up to comments, and a lively discussion followed.

This experiment proved very successful. It dispelled the secrecy of what was going on in the research group and demonstrated the genuine interest of the issues we discussed. The next year several people who had previously been hesitant joined the research group.

The research group discussions were immediate and practical, but they were also theoretical. We continually struggled with defining collaboration: what did it mean? Should we have shared meanings, or were diverse views to be encouraged? The questions were both epistemological (How do we know when we are collaborating?) and ethical (Is this a good way to proceed?). From all this talking we were moving toward some shared meanings and ethical norms to guide our relationships and work.

The research group was our richest and earliest example of talk that moved into dialogue. This context nourished learning across differences that created trust and strong relationships. Many of us have used our experience in these early discussions as a barometer for judging whether dialogue is occurring in other contexts. The dialogue in this group was the first context where I learned to trust openly expressing my opinion. I learned to trust the group and to feel that I could contribute without the undue influence of my assumed "power position." Many of us looked forward to these dialogues, even though a night at the end of the week and after a long meeting was an unlikely time to find such invigorating talk.

CONCLUSION

Six years of meetings is a lot of talking. It is in this talking, however, that we see learning and growth occurring. Lisa Westhoven, a clinical educator and co-coordinator of the PDS, in the round of interviews we did with everyone during the fourth year of the PDS, talked about the importance of dialogue.

LISA: Talking has made teaching much more interesting than it was before PDS. It's much more complex and much more of a thinking kind of profession than I thought it was. When I first started teaching, I think I did a lot of thinking about it. But then I didn't have anybody there to keep pushing me, and I think you can only think for yourself so much. You need somebody else to ask that next question, to get you over that next hump.

INTERVIEWER: A gentle sort of pushing?

LISA: Right, a little opening of a door to say, "Look in here," and then someone points to another door and says, "See? You missed this one over here."

INTERVIEWER: You didn't even know it was there.

LISA: That's what the PDS has provided for me—people to open the doors, people to ask questions that I couldn't have asked myself. If it hadn't been for the PDS, I don't think I would have stayed in teaching.

The productivity of our ongoing dialogue has helped us to realize how much we need our colleagues to keep us growing. However, talking across our differences, learning from them, and planning for the future has been both fruitful and difficult. The tensions created by our differences, by new roles and responsibilities, and by learning to rethink some of our beginning assumptions have led to a great deal of learning. But this learning has come at a price. It has pushed us to be self-critical risk-takers, and we have had to deal with the discomfort this sometimes creates. We have had to learn to talk to each other in new ways and to understand each other's professional contexts differently. We sometimes wonder if it is worth it; at other times we are convinced that it takes all this to support sustained professional growth.

The narratives, cases, and interpretations that follow are couched in persistent ambiguities. Learning to live in the tensions and on the borders of our institutional homes have been both tough and rewarding. I hope we have captured both our passion for what we are doing and the depth of what we have learned.

A Changing Forest

Mary Christenson

Mary Christenson, a clinical educator and second-grade teacher, uses the metaphor of a mature forest to examine her experience of the growth and development of the PDS. Her metaphor gave us an image that was helpful in reexamining our work together.

I visualize the PDS beginning as a barren field somewhere between the university and the schools. Now, with the somewhat random introduction of a variety of new species, it is on its way to becoming a mature forest.

There are many levels in a mature forest, from microscopic organisms in the subsoil to majestic trees in the upper canopy. Similarly, there are many levels in the PDS. All levels are important to the continued viability of the whole ecosystem. At the same time, the makeup of the forest and the PDS is constantly changing, both in large and small ways that can profoundly affect the natural balance. Some seeds land and flourish, while others grow quickly, then die or never sprout at all because they land among weeds or in rocky soil. Some teachers were looking for easy solutions to complex problems that did not come quickly. They flourished for a while in this environment but did not survive because they did not see their needs being met quickly enough. Other teachers chose to vacate the field because they came from schools where no one supported their efforts. As in the case of one species of plant competing with another, it was easier to vacate the field than to struggle against those who were trying to choke them out with negative attitudes and time pressures. Teachers and administrators who were not concerned with professional development through the PDS questioned and criticized the value of the PDS activities. They planned events that competed for the limited professional development time available, thus making PDS participation more difficult.

The perennials in our PDS forest are the teachers and faculty members who find this environment beneficial and choose to stay. They are not identical in appearance or needs, but they are persistent in their participation over a long enough period to have a significant impact on the nature of the environment. Eventually they grow to become part of the canopy layer of the forest. Like the large trees of a forest, they shelter and protect the new growth in the younger layers while maintaining the character of the entire forest.

The annual plants in our forest are the new teacher education students, our interns, who arrive every year. They are part of the annual cycle, and we know most will be gone at the end of our five-quarter program. With luck, they leave the forest able to transport the seeds of good educational practices to other places.

There are middle layers of plants in our forest as well. These are the GAs, who, while they have a time limit to their participation, may be around for more than one season. Their life cycles vary, but they contribute much to the texture and quality of our forest. They are at times able to give greater support and shelter to our annuals, because they are closer to both school and university than cooperating teachers or faculty members can be in their defined roles.

Soil, water, and sunshine are critical to the success of a forest. Our soil is the commitment to improving education for all students both young and old. Our water is the encouragement we get from others in the PDS. Sharing experiences has facilitated our growth in much the same way that plentiful rainfall benefits a forest after a drought. After being isolated in our classrooms for years, many of us have blossomed with a new excitement for teaching and learning because we meet regularly to discuss educational issues. Our sunshine is the hope that comes from new ideas. It brightens the future of education and helps us through the tough daily frustrations of teaching. It gives us the light needed to look reflectively at our teaching and at the larger picture and to visualize the possible long-term benefits of trying new things. Perennials that are successful in our forest may shelter and protect new growth, but they cannot give up their own soil, water, and light or they will not survive and the ecosystem will not thrive.

Our environment is changing because our PDS is taking a new direction this year. We have initiated a greater emphasis on professional growth for the cooperating teachers and university faculty. In recent years we have concentrated so much on our MEd interns that there has been little time for reflection or for refining our own practices. The expectation for personal reflection and change will alter the balance of our PDS forest's ecosystem. This change will undoubtedly be exciting for some and uncomfortable for others. Some plants will disappear and others will take their place. It is not the nature of a forest to try to accommodate all plants. Instead, those that flourish in the changing environment remain. Those that need other places to grow die out or produce seeds that are carried by natural means to new locations.

In a larger context, the fate of a forest, or a PDS, depends upon the rest of the world. If bureaucracies, in this case, school districts and universities, do not work together to help this venture flourish, we will again be faced with an empty field. We will again see only the uncomfortable distance that previously existed between university theory and classroom practice. Why should this happen? If there were no benefit in destroying rainforests, they would not be destroyed. The short-term benefits accrued to individuals cutting down the rainforests are causing long-term environmental problems for us all.

In the past, the distance between universities and schools probably benefited individuals in some way. Perhaps it maintained unnecessary jobs in two bureaucracies or supported delicate egos by creating a classroom system that allowed each group to consider its separate existence more important to education than the other. I do not know. But I believe that if this new common forest is clear cut from lack of institutional support, we are choosing short-term expediency over a longer-term approach to educational reform.

Without our forest, where do we find a truly common ground to share what each valuable participant knows about education?

CHAPTER 3

Our First Presentation: An Exhilarating Success and a Lingering Tension

Marilyn Johnston With PDS Participants

This chapter highlights the role of the individual in collaborative groups. When groups make collaborative decisions—in this case, about how to conduct a research presentation—does an individual have the right to make a personal decision counter to what the group has decided? What are the rights and responsibilities of an individual in a collaborative group?

We made our first presentation as a group in the fifth month of our first year. The college has an annual research conference each May and presentations are accepted after proposals are submitted. Then the college research committee organizes the one-day conference. Our proposal was accepted, and we spent six weeks preparing. A volunteer group met each week at Susi Long's house for pizza and to work on the presentation.

We were all quite anxious about this presentation. Our project was just beginning, and we had not done any systematic analysis of the video- and audiotapes we'd so religiously collected. The research group, which involved representatives from each of the schools, had done a lot of talking about collaboration, but no writing or presenting. A group of about 10 people volunteered to do the presentation; some were members of the research group.

PLANNING

Our first couple of "pizza meetings" (as our Tuesday planning sessions came to be called) were exciting but frustrating. We all had different ideas, or no idea, about what to do for this presentation. At the third meeting, we decided to go around the room and have each person say what he or she thought collaboration meant. We hoped our collective wisdom would give us a basis for the presentation. This went so well and was so interesting that we decided to organize our presentation as an informal conversation around issues related to collaboration. Most of our research work to date had taken place in similar conversations where we'd tried to address some definitional or problematic aspect of collaboration, so why not try to make the presentation work in this way? Most of the participants had never given a research presentation before and were leery of talking about research in front of an audience mostly of university professors and graduate students. Also, the typical format of one person at a time standing at a podium was not appealing to most of them. We decided that sticking to our usual way of talking together might make the presentation feel more comfortable to presenters and more authentic to the audience. On the other hand, straying from typical formats made Marilyn and the doctoral students nervous. We worried about whether the audience would be receptive to our unusual format.

Our conversational approach to research was an issue that required a lot of discussion. Most of the teachers and graduate students had traditional expectations for "research." Whether they had thought much about it or not, most thought of research as surveys, numbers, and proofs. Some of the graduate students had begun to take their qualitative research courses, and we had discussed these issues in our discussion group before the project had begun. A few teachers and some doctoral students, however, were anxious that what we were doing was not really research. I was aware that some of my faculty colleagues held similar opinions.

Our primary mode of research work had been conversation; we were learning through talking with each other. We had discussed at length different forms of data collection, and one of the graduate students or I videotaped or audiotaped all meetings. We had become quite comfortable with having the tape recorder or video camera on while we talked; there were occasional requests to turn them off while something sensitive was discussed. The data were piling up in my office, but no one had time to do a systematic analysis of it all. We occasionally transcribed a tape and passed it out to help us delve further into some issue. We had weekly journals from everyone in the PDS that we read together in the research group and tried to make sense of participant concerns. The journals stimulated a lot of talk and influenced how we conducted future Thursday night meetings. They helped us to be aware of an emerging set of divergent ideas within the group. Nevertheless, for this presentation, we did not have systematic results to report.

My influence during this planning process was probably strong. I tried to encourage a group decision-making process. I viewed the videotapes recently, and it is clear that my suggestions, while not offered frequently, were readily accepted. I was the only one who had presented before at a research conference. I had also had some previous experience with using experimental formats to represent collaborative processes in written texts and conference presentations (Cryns, Hunsaker, Johnston, Warshow & Weight, 1990;

Hunsaker & Johnston, 1992; Cryns & Johnston; 1993; Johnston, 1991). This group, however, felt much different than my previous work. The group was larger and the issues were in the early formative stages. So we struggled together to construct a presentation with a collaborative format, but I acknowledge my influence in these decisions.

THE PRESENTATION

For the actual presentation, we began with some short introductory comments to explain the organization of our PDS, one of the graduate students and I briefly spoke about our theoretical assumptions (a ploy at looking academically respectable), and then a third person gave a short description of and the reasons for our presentation format. The rest of the fifty-minute session was a simulated conversation on a problem in one of the schools we had not discussed before. We did not want to rehearse it ahead of time in order to make the conversation as authentic as possible. We practiced the introductory parts a lot, even going through them one more time right before our session. Everyone was nervous. Most would have been nervous anyway, but the experimental (and unscripted) nature of our presentation heightened the tension. The room was packed with more than 50 people. We looked different from the beginning. Rather than one person standing at the podium, we were four graduate students, two teachers, and one faculty person sitting in a semi-circle in the front.[1]

The presentation went well. The video camera quit after five minutes, so we didn't get the session recorded, but there were appreciative nods and good attention from the audience. About two-thirds of the way through the session, one of the graduate students, Paul Green, sensed a need to open up the floor to questions. A lively set of questions followed and the session was finally stopped by the conference organizer so that the next session could begin. There were many positive comments afterward and the presenting group took a glowing report back to the larger PDS group.

Overall, we felt very successful and also realized that we had learned a great deal by preparing for and giving this presentation. Preparation for presentations and writing for publication have been two of our most productive kinds of professional learning experiences.

THE TENSION

Paul's decision to open up the presentation to audience questions was followed by some intense debate because it raised some important issues about the tension between the rights of the individual and responsibilities to the group. We did not, however, at this point think about it as a productive tension. Mostly it seemed like a problem. There was a tendency in the beginning, although not for all, to think of the group as the site for collaboration and individual prerogatives as outside collaboration. This position, however, obviated a productive tension between the individual and the group. When Paul made an individual decision during the presentation, it raised the question of whether collaboration allows for this kind of individual initiative without seeking feedback from the group.

The conversations following the presentation were not easy. Two people in the presentation group talked with Paul individually and we scheduled a debriefing meeting with the research group, which we would have done regardless of Paul's decision to change the presentation format. Paul felt he'd been put on the spot and criticized even as others assured him that this was not intended. The fact that everyone felt the presentation was very successful helped, but it probably was not easy for him to be the example at the center of attention when the presentation was discussed.

In the dialogue that follows, we are struggling with this issue, and it is clear that we have different opinions and work from different assumptions. This incident helped us to work through and raise further questions about our emerging collaborative norms.

THE DEBRIEFING CONVERSATION

What follows is an edited version of part of the debriefing session held a week after the presentation. The group included the presentation group as well as other members of the research group. The conversation was edited from a transcript made from the videotape of the meeting. The conversation captures the diverse opinions of the research group and raises issues that plagued us for some time.

PAUL (GA): I'd like to hear what you all have to say.
ROSARIO (CT): I think it was good. You opened it up and it was for the benefit of the group, including the audience.
LISA (CT): It was also risky for the audience; the audience response, it could have turned out differently—it could have been awful.
PAUL: That's true.
RICK (GA): If you're planning something as a group, how can you determine when the individual can step in and divert what the group has decided it wanted to do?

ROSARIO: I think as long as the intent is for the benefit of the group, then it's okay; even if it doesn't turn out good, the intent is good. Maybe Paul began something for his own purposes but then it turned out okay. I would still want to call Paul on that because I thought it was for his own ego, not for the group. Or if he did something that was for the benefit of the group, but it didn't turn out so well, I would still think it was okay because it benefited the group.

PAUL: What I did made it so that Jeff couldn't do his planned chunk. It circumvented that. I didn't even think about that until Rick and I had a long conversation afterward. It's a complicated issue.

JEFF (GA): My feeling was that it benefited the group and the presentation came out a lot better than I anticipated because I had so many uncertainties about it.

PAUL: If we're actually trying to give a fairly faithful simulation of our process, what happens is that people speak up and things like that.

RICK: But I think that we didn't allow ourselves that option. We talked about whether to leave it open ended and we decided to be very definite about what was going to happen. For me the whole thing is about individual initiative.

PAUL: This time we decided not to have that choice—of an individual having the right to change the conversation.

JEFF: That's because we had the time frame.

ROSARIO: The audience was ready for questions.

MARILYN: They had lots of questions.

PAUL: We had decided not to have a question-and-answer period.

MARILYN: But then you reversed that group decision.

PAUL: That's the question.

RICK: The question in my mind is not whether it worked out well—I don't think anyone denies the fact that what happened worked out—but rather, where does the individual play a role?

ROSARIO: If the individual doesn't have any rights, then I think we get down to the lowest common denominator.

MARILYN: But what kinds of rights? Maybe the issue, as Rick and Rosario have said, is about the right of the individual. If we've planned to do something like a presentation, and we have in mind what we are going to do, should any of us in that situation feel free to do something that they feel is apropos to the moment?

RICK: I think the question is not just about presentations, but where does the individual play a role in the collaborative process in general?

MARILYN: I didn't mean to exclude that. It's just that personally I did not feel like it was a productive thing to do, because all of a sudden we had people barraging us with questions, and Paul and I were the only ones responding to them. I felt put on the spot because they were asking questions we hadn't dealt with in the group. How are you going to write up your research? How are you going to write collaboratively? We haven't talked about those issues yet. I was trying very hard in planning the presentation not to be the "boss," not to talk too much, so I felt like it put me in a situation that I didn't want to be in.

SUSI: I felt that definitely. When one of the questions was asked, I felt like, *whoosh*, right in Marilyn's direction. A lot of us did.

PAUL: So when you said it wasn't productive, are you saying it wasn't good?

MARILYN: No, I was saying that I felt uncomfortable.

PAUL: So it wasn't good. That's what I was wondering. What was it not productive of?

MARILYN: Maybe not productive of a collaborative process. It felt like all of a sudden we weren't in a collaborative group, we were in traditional roles.

ROSARIO: If they'd asked something about the school or the teachers' role, then I could have answered.

JEFF: I would hope we'd all be well versed enough to respond.

MARILYN: Then why were Paul and I the only ones answering the questions? Did we shut others out, or not wait long enough?

SUSI: We all have an opinion about things, and most of the questions weren't necessarily heavy-duty questions. We probably turned to you, but maybe you two also assumed that you were the proper persons to answer.

MARILYN: I didn't know how to negotiate it. Maybe I could have said, "Does anyone want to answer that?"

PAUL: It was on the spot, and wait time is difficult.

ROSARIO: I didn't even realize that you were answering all the questions— not at all.

PAUL: After thinking about what happened in the presentation, what I've come down to is that it didn't fit with the way we had planned. It went against the group's decision, and it did take the floor away from everybody else, but also it was collaborative because it was an action based on my best sense, my own best sense, of what our group process was leading toward. But it was offered in not a very good way because it couldn't be discussed in that setting. I could have brought it up in a way that would have made it possible for someone to say, "No, I don't think we should." And I didn't do that, but if we somehow come up with a way that dogmatically rules out that kind of initiative for more successful presentations, then I think it reflects poorly on collaboration, and I think it has consequences for the role of the individual in a collaboration. If we're actually trying to make how we present and who is included match the norms of the greater collaboration and then we set in abeyance the most important ones, then I think there's a conflict there.

SUSI: I think about the nature of presentations. It's not a real meeting; it's a simulation of it. Even though there was some real conversation going on, it was formal.

MARILYN: In a presentation, maybe the collaboration comes *before* and *after* but not *during*. Maybe we can't use a collaborative process in the middle of the process—or maybe we could have asked the group to make the decision right there.

PAUL: Then we shouldn't claim that we are simulating collaboration. For someone to take notice of the need for questions during the course of the presentation and have that person not be able to speak would be unfortunate.

ROSARIO: You were reading the audience cues.

PAUL: They were pretty obvious, too.

ROSARIO: They were chomping at the bit.

SUSI: I wonder what would have happened if Paul had said, "It really looks like there are lots of questions," and Rick had said, "But Jeff has something that he planned to say at the end," but Jeff had said, "That's okay, let's go on"—we would have gotten into this whole discussion, then.

JEFF: Even if that had happened, we still would have put Marilyn on the spot.

RICK: The thing it did was establish a hierarchy that we want to claim doesn't exist.

LISA: If we'd had a different audience, the questions would have been different.

ROSARIO: More practical, front-line questions.

BELVA (classroom teacher): If they're going to ask a question about what's going on in the classroom, that's where we're more comfortable because that's what we deal with.

MARILYN: Maybe I have to work on not feeling responsible for answering the questions.

RICK: Even the fact that we're having this conversation, should that situation arise in the future and someone says, "I think we should open it up," I think we will know then how we feel about these issues. We won't need to go through this long conversation because we've laid the groundwork.

This incident (and the conversations following) were provocative. We have come back to it time and time again. It's become a gauge against which we have judged many other situations in a process of defining what the collaborative "zone" will be. It seems that such norms must be established in practice, not a priori. Without this critical incident, an incident we have not been able to judge to be collaborative or non-collaborative, we would have had less rich discussions, less complex struggles, and less clear understandings of collaboration.

SOME RETROSPECTIVE REFLECTIONS: PAUL AND MARILYN

Paul and Marilyn did some informal writing about this incident and some time later they began to write together for a published article which was never finished. Paul's writing begins a couple months after the presentation and then a year later:

> By the time a week had passed, I had plenty of time to inflate my anxiety over the matter to the proportions of a Macy's Thanksgiving Day parade balloon. My stomach tied into knots as I heard our "chief worrier," the OSU faculty member [Marilyn], pronounce her judgment of my action as "not productive." Others had seen the action as beneficial, but the way we (or I) positioned the faculty member at this meeting added great weight to her disagreement. I felt mortally wounded and considered leaving the collaboration. I was also confused as to whether or not an individual can or should act as I did in a collaboration. Was I collaborative in our presentation? Was I collaborative at all? Was membership in this project worth the gut-wrenching process of evaluative reflection? (July 1992)

A year later, Paul is more analytic about the issues, but his memories of his choices and feelings are still strong:

> Over the months preceding the research conference presentation, we had come to view ourselves as collaborators. Although never reaching a shared ideal, our collaboration had begun bridging the distance separating the university from the schools in the project. Our tentative sense of ourselves as a group of collaborators began finally to gel into a body of shared meanings and jointly held beliefs about what people ought to do in collaborations like ours. . . . We came up with a kind of "collaborative zone" within which we tried to operate as we became less insecure in it. In this way, a collaborative culture began to

emerge, and we did our best to continually locate ourselves and our project within it.

An inevitable consequence of demarcating such a "zone" is that occasionally, especially under stressful or unfamiliar circumstances, we will act in such a way as to land outside it. The dramatic tension of our research presentation story was stimulated from the question of how collaborators will deal with that kind of event. Having stumbled into the frontier, outside the relatively well-mapped, civilized territory of the prior history of our collaboration, we needed to decide whether to annex the new territory or to mark it off limits. Either way, we needed to make sense of it.

If we were to leave the territory of my act outside our zone of collaboration, that would lead to one family of interpretations. At best, it may have been a mistake—a miscue, or the act of an impulsive, jittery novice presenter. At worst, it might have been showmanship of a most uncollaborative kind, drawing the spotlight away from others for the mere pleasure of the attention gained. Depending on how much I was identified with this act, I, too, felt I could have been left outside the "zone." (The risk I felt was actually like that of a potential exile, banished from the collaborative zone to the territory I opened up but which wasn't found suitable for cultivation. This risk was personal and personally felt. While other opportunities for research for graduate students were available to me, my investment in the project had become very strong.) But on the other hand, if the new territory could be interpreted to be collaborative, it could be annexed, and I with it. (March 1992)

Paul and Marilyn talked and wrote about the presentation and its related issues for some time. Marilyn's writing is also a mixture of feelings and analysis:

I felt very conflicted during the conversations following the presentation. During the debriefing conversation, I was juggling two concerns. The first was my friendship with Paul and my sense that as a first-year doctoral student he was struggling with his own sense of security and definition. His public appearance and abilities to express himself articulately belied a sense of uncertainty that I did not want to exacerbate.

The second concern was a kind of protective attitude toward the collaborative project. The project was less than five months old to the teachers in the project. The doctoral students had been around since the summer, so their participation extended almost a year. Because the graduate students and I had been talking about collaboration longer, I was afraid that we would dominate the presentation, and sure enough, we did—or at least, Paul and I did.

I was surprised that the teachers were pleased with the question-and-answer time. Even the doctoral student and teacher who did not get to do their parts because of the questioning seemed genuinely unperturbed. They had come to all the planning sessions and then didn't get to do their part. Maybe they felt relieved. It was a big audience; it was their first such presentation. Actually, all of us had the jitters beforehand. (May 1991)

Looking at the videotape of the debriefing conversation some eight months later, Marilyn thinks about her own role in influencing the direction of the discussion:

I remember during the discussion that I wanted to raise questions about Paul's opening up the discussion. Was I doing this to encourage dialogue, or had I had already decided that this was not a collaborative move? In watching the tape eight months later, I see myself pushing the discussion toward an idealistic definition of collaboration—that is, working as a group, making group decisions, and negotiating changes. In the process of conducting this debriefing situation, Paul's feelings are somewhat sacrificed for the sake of the emerging norms of collaboration. (January 1992)

CONCLUSION

Paul's example has spirited many conversations about the complex interaction of the individual with the collaborative group. The anguish of Paul's decision was no doubt exacerbated by the rather strong position Marilyn took as she tried to nurture emerging collaboration norms. Had this experience occurred later in the project, it probably would have received only passing attention. In the beginning, however, we had not figured out how to both validate individual initiative and retain collaborative norms.

Through many conversations, we have come to understand that the individual and group must be held in a productive tension. If the group overrides individual initiative, it loses the potential for critique and variation that only autonomous individuals can provide. If the individual has insufficient responsibility and attachment to the group, there can be no collaboration.

We no longer consider individual decisions to be in conflict with collaboration, but in a tension that requires constant monitoring. We must be vigilant as to how decisions get made, what motivates them, and whether our conversations about decisions are open to differences and critique. It is simpler to choose group cohesion or individual autonomy than to try to keep the tension. And maybe as our collaborative group was forming we needed more emphasis on the group, whereas with more history and trust we can now sustain more individual initiative. However, the tendency of groups to ward off critique and differences is as great as the individual's potential to destroy community. Both require at times that we do what we are least inclined to do.

Our only salvation is constant conversation of the sort we had about our presentation. These kinds of dialogues help us learn about ourselves as we participate in a community that requires both our support and our willingness to challenge it.

NOTE

1. The presenters included Paul Green, Jeff Smith, Rick Kerper, and Susi Long (GAs); Rosario Galarza and Lisa Westhoven (classroom teachers); and Marilyn Johnston (faculty).

Alert! Hurricane Status

Donna Weatherholtz

Donna Weatherholtz was a doctoral student and GA in the PDS for two years. In this metaphor she sees similarities between her experience and a hurricane alert. The chapters before and after this interlude describe similar metaphoric hurricanes that caused large waves of issues and feelings as PDS participants struggled to deal with the changing landscape of a developing PDS.

Almost everyone is fascinated by hurricanes. Some are hurricane hunters who track storms and travel to storm sites to experience the awesome power and thrill of the dangerous risks involved. Others, like me, start packing, boarding up residences, tying down anything that is loose, and stocking up on supplies. Still others evacuate.

Participating in this PDS project is much like going through a hurricane. I will call it Hurricane PDS. In this metaphor, I vacillate between being a hurricane hunter and being an evacuator.

I see Hurricane PDS coming in my direction and I am struck by the imposing power of it. I want the information and learning that can occur as the winds of collaboration rise. And as collaboration reaches storm and gale-force winds, the excitement of the opportunity for personal change also increases the risk of personal pain. I want to be there to experience Hurricane PDS, but many times I do not want to get close enough to participate in the interaction. The hurricane by its very nature requires the openness and the willingness of its participants to be vulnerable. This brings with it the risk of pain.

Participating in small group discussions is a safe place for me. However, the large-group participation brings out my packing, boarding-up, and tying-down behaviors, signaling that I am getting too close to Hurricane PDS. To share and disclose personal opinions in the large group evinces the torrential rains of fear that accompany the hurricane. The fear of getting damaged sends me scurrying to the nearest shelter, but then Hurricane PDS entices me to get close to the collaboration again.

A few of my cohorts, the hurricane hunters, have traveled to the eye of the storm. This is a tenuous journey at best. As often as I move into the hurricane, I get tossed back by the gale-force winds. Sometimes it feels like I am drowning in the raging sea.

As I talk the language of collaboration, I am drawn closer to the eye of the storm. As soon as I recognize incongruence in myself, I run away from the hurricane. Yet I eagerly want the information, the knowledge, and the excitement of the power of collaboration. What will the cleanup-and-repair phase of my collaborative change bring? What will my inquiry into my own espoused beliefs bring? The personal changes so far have created ten-foot waves climbing and crashing on my old belief systems. Hurricane PDS is changing me.

Before the storm winds reach hurricane strength, I must decide if I will be a hurricane hunter, striving for the eye of the storm, or a hurricane evacuator, packing up and tying down. The experience continues to be awe inspiring as well as risky.

CHAPTER 4

Rethinking Our Roles

Richard M. Kerper and Marilyn Johnston

In this chapter, Marilyn (university professor) and Rick (doctoral student) discuss the changes in their understandings of the power issues related to their university roles. We began with romanticized views about ignoring our university roles and giving up the power ascribed to them in order to promote collaboration and empower the teachers. We have to rethink our roles as we find that trying to give up power does not empower teachers as much as it limits our ability to participate collaboratively. Likewise, Rick, as a GA in one of the PDS schools, tries to "become part of the school culture." The frustrations that ensue from this romanticized expectation lead him to rethink his role in the school as well.

In this chapter we use metaphors from the field of journalism to talk about our roles in this project. (For a more developed paper on two related issues—parity and power—see Johnston & Kerper, 1996.) Using these metaphors, we trace the changes in our thinking related to our university roles in our collaborative project. We write in separate narratives in order to show the differences in our perspectives and experience. While we both were "from the university," we were positioned differently and/or positioned ourselves in ways that challenged our thinking about our roles. Our separate narratives also allow us to point to the power issues between professors and graduate students working collaboratively. Marilyn's narrative comes first because her historical account provides a context for Rick's discussion of his role.

BEGINNING ASSUMPTIONS

We began with a traditional conception of institutional roles. On this view, roles are static, formal, and ritualistic; individuals occupy roles that designate their predetermined position in a social structure (Nisbet, 1970). This static understanding of role does not account for the ways we position or are positioned by others in different contexts. Assuming that we could "give up" our roles was a view that ignored the social construction of roles and the linguistic basis of their construction (Davies & Harré, 1990). Our initial static view of roles was challenged by our colleagues as we were positioned in traditional roles in spite of our deliberate intentions to de-position ourselves.

Concurrently with this view, we saw the hierarchy implied by traditional role definitions between universities and schools to be antithetical to the equity, parity, and mutuality required for collaboration (Clift, Veal, Holland, Johnson, & McCarthy, 1995; Zimpher, 1990). If university roles were ascribed more power and influence than school-based roles, it seemed obvious to us that this would interfere with collaboration. We had to rethink what equity, parity, and mutuality meant in light of reconstructed definitions of a role.

Rethinking our roles has required many conversations with our school colleagues and with each other. Our actions based on these initial assumptions prompted problems and frustrations that forced us to rethink our positionings and assumptions about them. Without these cross-institutional interactions, and particularly our ongoing conversations about them, we likely would have remained either unaware of our power positionings or unable to reconstruct them on our own.

ACADEMIC ASIDE: INSTITUTIONAL ROLES

The traditional conception of role, according to Davies and Harré (1990), is problematic because it does not account for the ways in which our positions in the world are linguistically and socially constructed. They argue that our positions in the social world are in the process of continually being constructed within conversations. How we position ourselves relative to the discursive positions available to us accounts for our view of reality:

> Once having taken up a particular position as one's own, [whether consciously or not,] a person inevitably sees the world from the vantage point of that position and in terms of the particular images, metaphors, story lines, and concepts which are made relevant within the particular discursive practice in which they are positioned. (p. 46)

As we began this project, we were critical of the traditional images and concepts that grounded school/university relations; we wanted to change our roles. A colleague gave us a paper by Davies and Harré's on their concept of "positioning." We found this idea helpful because it provided a theoretical stance that explained the fluid and even contradictory positionings in which we found ourselves. Traditional role theories could not explain the fluidity and changeability of our practical experience.

Their use of feminist post-structural theories deconstructs the general definition of institutional roles that are determined by one's position in an institution to meanings that are constructed through language in social situations. The former generalizes across contexts; the latter is dependent on discourses that are linguistically and historically situated.

Davies and Harré (1990) also point to interpretive issues and the ways in which we can be only partially aware of our own intentions and the meanings of others. They speak of persons living in different narratives and thus having difficulty participating in each other's stories. They argue that "two people can be living quite different narratives without realizing that they are doing so" (p. 57). The consequence may be misunderstandings.

The idea of living in different narratives helped us theorize how we understood and intended our positionings and how we were positioned by others in the project. Sometimes our misunderstandings led to conflict or frustration, but they were also the fruitful ground from which we were forced/helped to rethink our roles.

MARILYN'S ROLES

I use the metaphor of jobs within a news publication because it allows me to situate myself in several different roles as well as emphasize the important role of communication and discourse within our project.

An Advertiser

My initial role in this project was like being in the advertising department. Advertising is the economic lifeblood of a news publication, to sustain both its budget and its readership. Similarly, I played two kinds of advertising roles in our project. I solicited funding to get the project started (I wrote for grant monies to support the project) and then recruited help in advertising our collaborative project. The doctoral students and I created a beginning advertisement. The project was to be a curricular project related to the 1992 Columbian Quincentenary. This was an attractive focus for both funders and potential participants because the celebration of the quincentenary of Christopher Columbus's encounters in the Americas was a lively and controversial topic in Columbus, Ohio. As a social studies educator, I was interested in teachers rethinking and reconstructing the stereotypic hero stories related to Christopher Columbus in order to give students a wider and more multicultural view of this historical period. To attract both funding and participants, the project was packaged as one to develop schools as demonstration sites for tourists visiting Columbus in 1992 (many were expected).

As with most well-designed advertisements, it had its fine print, which stated that the process to develop these projects would involve collaborative work between schools, and between the schools and the university. For some, this fine print was probably interpreted much like the health warnings on many products. As with most health hazards, potential users did not really know or care much about collaboration, but it probably was something best done without. Given such warnings, one has to decide whether the benefits (school projects) are worth the risks (time and the unknown challenges of working collaboratively).

Advertisements also have hidden assumptions and values, as did ours. While the packaging looked quite attractive and appeared to be consonant with the tourist-oriented focus of the Quincentenary more broadly, the values of both the curriculum and the collaboration were anti-institutional. There was an implicit critique of traditional textbook accounts of Christopher Columbus in the first case as well as a critique of the hierarchical and unequal power relations typical of school and university associations. The packaging looked conventional; the underlying values were critical of those conventions.

As we were developing our advertisement and strategies for the project, we tried them out in some school settings. Typically, one of the doctoral students and I met with a principal and some of the staff. We tried out our "pitch" and watched carefully for feedback; we used the feedback to reorient how we talked to the next school group in order to make our presentation as effective as possible.

My strongest memory of my advertising role was of our first meeting with the schools who agreed to work with us. I was quite tense. Even though people were there because they had decided to join the project, it felt like the first meeting would set the tone for our future work. I recounted a version of the recruitment story they had heard before. I described where the funding had come from, what I hoped we would accomplish, and how we would try to work together. While this "presentation" felt very powerful because everyone listened attentively, I was acutely aware of the contradictions. What I wanted most was to de-position myself from a primary leadership role, and here I was, standing in front of the group, advocating for the direction and means by which we would work together.

Rick got up next and described the research project. If an advertisement for collaboration was on shaky ground, an advertisement for a research project was analogous to selling something no one felt they needed. We persisted out of commitment rather than because of its attractiveness to our clients. Rick explained that we wanted a teacher or two from each building to help us study the evolution of our collaboration. He acknowledged that none of us knew much about working collaboratively, and that watching it carefully would help us adapt things as we went along. There were few questions about either of our "pitches."

From the beginning there was excitement about the school projects and the potential for attracting visitors to project schools. In contrast, proposals for collaboration and research were met with skepticism. The contrast in reception pointed to the wide divide between the school and university participants' early understandings and expectations. Just because they had decided to join didn't mean they understood or cared about either research or collaboration. It's more likely that they decided the risks were worth taking in order to have the positive aspects—the projects.

My advertising role in the project raised many questions for me. It was easy to invite teachers into the curricular aspects of the projects. I cared about this kind of work and was willing to support them in their projects. In contrast, I had a heavy conscience about trying to sell collaboration and research. As the salesperson, I knew that I was not only advocating for processes and work that were of little interest to most of them, but that my advertising role was counterproductive to the very collaborative processes I wanted to establish.

My role in these respects was continually under scrutiny. This was partly because I kept raising the topic; I was often uncomfortable with the ways I got positioned and maybe also with the ways I positioned myself. The role of designing the advertisement, both what and how it would be done, is similar to the power typically ascribed to university participants in school/university projects. They have a product—a new way of teaching math, a new curriculum for social studies, or research findings that suggest changes in teaching. They then try to sell their product to teachers. Teachers rarely get a voice in whether they will adopt these programs because most programs are mandated by administrators. Teachers, however, decide whether or not to use them in their classrooms, which gives them the ultimate power in determining their success. I was convinced that the typical hierarchical mandates of these types were antithetical to collaboration.

Part of my distress was fueled by a rather romanticized view of collaboration. I thought that in order to address the power inequities, I should "give up" or "give over" the authority associated with my institutional role. My goal was group power and shared collaborative norms. I was unclear about how this might be accomplished, but I felt certain that exercising too much authority would be detrimental.

I was not then making a distinction between authority and leadership which might have helped me sort through some of the other positional choices I could have taken. Defining my role primarily in terms of negative power issues clouded an understanding of the positive potential that a leadership role has—it can be used to support a collaborative process. At the time, leadership and authority were both seen as negative and in opposition to more collaborative norms of collegiality and equity.

Even if I was ready to share my individual power and work more collaboratively, the doctoral students seemed initially uneasy with this, and subsequently many of the teachers were equally uncomfortable. Working with the doctoral students gave me some initial clues as to how difficult this would be. A couple of the doctoral students were comfortable with new relationships, but most talked about feeling vulnerable with a professor they anticipated would give them grades, sit on examination committees, and advise their dissertations. It was hard to trust relations that countered institutional norms and expectations.

Also, we typically were struggling with very complex topics (e.g., the nature of collaboration, the meaning of mutuality and parity); the level of ambiguity was high. There were not ready solutions to these kinds of puzzles, and translating them into practice presented even further intellectual challenges. Some of the doctoral students felt at risk, lest they look unintelligent to me or to each other. It was hard to imagine how we could reach a sense of trust and parity under these conditions.

As new teachers joined us, we began anew to raise questions about our roles and relationships. My approach to de-positioning myself was to avoid answering questions or making decisions as often as I could. This caused much frustration in the beginning because it countered teachers' expectations and created ambiguity about where we were going. Nevertheless, the issues about my role meant that we began talking about how to do things differently.

A Reporter

As the project expanded during the first year, I found myself operating as a reporter, moving from one committee or small group to another, carrying reports of what had gone on somewhere else. By the end of the first quarter, each of the school groups was organized and into planning their curricular projects. I worked closely with one school; doctoral students paired up with the other schools to help plan their curricular project. We also got the research group started and had one or more volunteer teachers from each school meeting weekly. At the end of the second quarter we were designated by the university as a professional development school (PDS)—this added a teacher education reform agenda, and by the third quarter we had a cohort of 24 master's of education certification students placed in teachers' classrooms. We decided to create a steering committee that met weekly to facilitate planning and to bring proposals for decision making back to the group.

My role expanded with the project. As we designed more and more groups to handle different responsibilities, I found myself at more and more meetings. I was the only person who went to all of the weekly meetings—steering committee, research group, doctoral students' discussion group, and Thursday evening whole group meeting; and in addition, my school group had decided to have a Tuesday meeting. There was also a weekly seminar with the MEd interns to discuss their issues.

Day after day I went from one meeting to the next, often reporting on what had happened in a previous meeting. Carrying reports from one group to another meant I played a major interpretive role. The traditional conception of a reporter is of someone who reports objectively on what has happened; the reporter is merely a recorder of a story as it "really" happened. My experience, along with the opinions of a host of theorists, would suggest otherwise. (See chapter 7 for further discussion of these issues.) I was well aware of the interpretive power I held. No matter how careful I was, I knew that my biases were operating. I wanted the project to move toward collaborative norms and processes and was no doubt supporting this goal in the way I carried stories from one group to another.

My participation in this process took me beyond the typical reporter role because I was (am) a participant as well. I had a voice in the decision making, along with others. The fact that I was reporting to other groups on these decisions made my dual role of reporter and participant even more powerful.

At times the work I was doing felt very productive, yet at other times I felt distressed by the power I continued to hold in shaping the project. I was eager for a more shared sense of ownership, and my reporter role seemed to get in the way of this. An early entry in my journal recounts an example of this:

> It is only the fourth week of the quarter but the [certification] students are very frustrated with having to attend Thursday night meetings. They think they are being asked to do too many things that do not relate directly to their courses and fieldwork. I took their frustration to the steering committee on Tuesday. I tried to recount their arguments as best I could, but I also knew that my interest (i.e., involving them in Thursday nights so they will see how decisions are made) colored how I presented it. We decided to take it to the Thursday night meeting and have the group discuss it. I had already agreed at the seminar that the students could skip this Thursday because they have a big project due on Friday. The Thursday group decided to have them come every other week, and I communicated that to the students after class on Friday. Most of them seemed satisfied. Going from group to group, carrying these issues and problems, is very interesting, but I am constantly aware of the power that it gives me. (October 1991)

While I was aware of shaping stories as I carried them from group to group, I was also cognizant that I could be only partly aware of how my interests were influencing my actions and the perceptions of others. When I was aware of this influence, it raised ethical questions for me. I often took my worries about this to the doctoral students or research group meetings for their analyses and suggestions. Was I too controlling? Was I inserting my perspective too directly? Was I allowing others to make decisions? Their responses were helpful—sometimes supportive, at other times critical. They did not always agree with each other, but the discussions helped me critically examine my actions.

In this reporter role, I was positioning myself in a place of authority because I carried reports from one group to another. At the same time, I knew if I took too much responsibility for this that it would limit the collaboration. On the other hand, I was concerned about shaping the project in a collaborative way. There was an inherent contradiction in policing a set of the norms in order to ensure its collaborative nature. I was perplexed by how to move from the role of reporting to one of constructing a shared story.

By the end of the first eighteen months, my role as reporter had had some unanticipated outcomes. As I went from one discussion to another, I was changing my mind about many things. What I was learning was gradually influencing how I participated and how I thought about my participation. For example, there were some differences within my school group, between the teachers and the principal, that developed the first year. The collaborative decision making had given the teachers a sense of empowerment; the principal was only marginally supportive of this. Consequently, when he was around, they were hesitant to speak up but then unhappy that they couldn't. I found that I could say things that the teachers wanted said without negative repercussions because I was not subject to his authority in the same way. In addition, because of my university role, my comments seemed to carry more authority than when the teachers said the same thing. It was my voice telling the story, but it was their message.

At first I thought this was uncollaborative; I was using my institutional authority to speak in their place. My goal was to be a "member of a collaborative group," not the voice of authority. What the teachers helped me to understand was that in this situation I was making a positive contribution to mutual goals rather than robbing them of authority. From this example and others, I slowly began to see my simple version of "I should get out of authoritative positions" as an inflexible and unhelpful stance. Such a stance actually limited my ability to support our collaboration.

In the research group, my reporter role was very different. Here teachers, doctoral students, Rick, and I met together weekly and more often when we were getting ready for a conference presentation or writing a paper. This was the first place where we actually felt a sense of parity. By parity, we meant a mutual respect for everyone's perspective and for differing expectations and expertise. We were a smaller group (12 participants or so). We spent a lot of time together, including traveling to conferences, and we talked regularly about the difficulties of trying to work collaboratively. We analyzed what was working in each school group, talked about the difficulties as they arose, puzzled about how norms got established, and critiqued the influence of institutional roles on what we were doing.

In this group there were many reporters and many points of view. My opinions were valued no more or less than anyone else's. Teachers were telling stories about their situations and issues they were puzzling about. In these cases, they were reporters with an insider's perspective; they were the experts and creators of their own stories. The rest of the group asked questions, made suggestions, and provided support, but each reporter was positioned as the authority on her or his own experience and each of us had his or her own turn.

We were also creating some shared stories. We were coming to some understandings of what collaboration would be in this project, what expectations we would hold for each other and ourselves, and the norms that would guide our relationships. Telling our own stories helped to create shared stories.

I learned a lot about the benefits and burdens of my university role from these many conversations. From these analyses I have reconsidered my initial assumptions about collaboration and my role in it. I have come to understand collaboration as a much more ambiguous and fluid process than I initially anticipated. I have also come to expect that the shifts in positioning will be both challenging and intriguing. I no longer hold to a simple view that I must "give up" the authority ascribed to my institutional role; at times authority can be useful, either for leadership purposes or for political objectives. My questions now are more about the uses of authority and whether or not they contribute to building relationships and furthering collaborative goals than avoiding leadership positionings. The question of power is not one to be given away or simply avoided. Rather, I have learned from my colleagues that the ways we talk to each other and build shared relationships are more important than who is positioned in what role at what time. I have come to appreciate how leadership and collegiality are most productive when kept in a productive tension.

I have also become acutely aware of the limited nature of my own thinking. Even as I find new understandings, I realize that these are incomplete and fluid, because of the limits of my ability to know my own thoughts and because the project itself is evolving. I am also convinced that for all my good intentions and reflections, I can be only partly aware of my own ideas, and much less of how I am understood by others. Further, some of these issues have become irrelevant as new school and university people join the project with other interests and concerns. I occasionally wonder whether we are slipping back into more hierarchical relationships and whether the same issues and concerns need to be raised again. If I raised these questions, how would I do this differently, based on what I have learned in the past? Or do we need to move on to other questions?

An Editor

Flexible positionings and mutual respect prompt a range of reports and stories by many authors. As participants have come to assert more freely their own points of view and stories than was true in the beginning, my role has changed. Sometimes I still play a reporter's role, but so do others. Sometimes I write my own story. At other times we write stories together. And yet we have new members who are feeling tentative and intimidated by the institutional role I represent.

As I sit writing this book, I am intrigued by this diversity as well as by the many ways we have communicated ideas and perspectives with each other. Some find that dialogue with others best prompts their thinking; others prefer writing at the computer; still others focus on inquiry in their classrooms or work with interns; others are more concerned with processes of planning and shaping our collaboration. My role takes on an editorial function as I try to mold the activities, interests, ideas, and learnings into a book so we can communicate with others.

As I take on this role, I have assumed a different kind of power that provokes continued reflection. How do I position myself as an editor and still support a collaborative process? How do I maintain a productive tension between my own perspective and the differing voices of my colleagues? How do I deal with the criticism that writing a book is tugging teachers into university territory rather than supporting their concerns and voices within the norms and expectations of school cultures? These are not questions for which I expect to find answers. They are tensions that keep me alert to issues of power, and as such, feed the questioning that keeps my present role as editor a lively intellectual endeavor.

By my earlier definition of collaboration, my present editor's role would have failed to qualify as a collaborative task. Now I see myself holding a temporary role in order to facilitate a particular collaborative effort. I have a sabbatical leave to do the writing; my institutional context both expects and supports this kind of effort. For teachers, their school contexts neither support nor reward writing. The opportunity for others to participate at varied levels gives me the opportunity to position myself in this role.

Of course, this more flexible and fluid sense of my participation does not settle the power issues related to my university role any more than my earlier romantic notions did. I am aware, as I was earlier, that I exercise a great deal of power as I make editorial decisions. I try to keep my biases and influence as points of tension to be questioned as best I can, but again I acknowledge the impossibility of doing this in any satisfactory way.

RICK'S ROLES

In this section, I tell the story of my doctoral student experience within a school/university collaborative project. I use the metaphor of jobs within broadcast journalism to capture the dynamic nature of my role. It allows me to capture the evolving role that I constructed with others in the project, a role in which I was influenced and influential, controlled and controlling.

A Broadcast Journalism Student

I began my involvement with the collaborative project like a student in a broadcast journalism course who wants to learn about the field. I wanted to learn about school/university collaboration. I had taken a course on collaboration with Marilyn that rekindled my passion for working *with* teachers, not *on* teachers. Within this university context I felt like a novice, a learner. I assumed that Marilyn had an understanding of collaboration that I could discover if I listened and watched carefully enough. So in addition to my coursework and my graduate assistant responsibilities, I volunteered to participate in the project. I sat in weekly meetings with other doctoral students interested in collaboration and listened to the unfolding conversation, hoping to discover the norms that Marilyn held for collaborative work. When I asked questions, I positioned Marilyn as the expert and Paul, one of the other doctoral students, as more knowledgeable than I. On occasion I tentatively voiced my thoughts. However, if they were not embraced by the group, I listened even more closely, figuring that I had not yet uncovered the collaborative norms of the project.

Within the university environment I felt vulnerable. Although Marilyn tried to deal with me as an equal partner in the project, the hierarchy of the institution reminded me of the power differential between student and professor. As the professor of courses in which I enrolled, Marilyn evaluated my thinking. As project director she controlled opportunities for employment. As a member of my general examination committee, she could affect the completion of my degree. And after my graduation, her recommendation could influence my marketability within higher education. In the same way that journalism students might feel at risk studying disciplines in which they are not fully confident of their abilities, I felt surrounded by uncertainty and risk. I approached the venture with trepidation and at the same time an overriding belief that I could learn from it.

A New Staff Writer

I continued my involvement in the collaborative project with the uncertainty of a newly hired staff writer for a broadcast news program. I was grateful to be on the team, but I was uncertain about my role. I had jumped at the opportunity to participate in the project and once more to be linked to a school community. I thought this project provided more, though. I believed it would enable me to become bicultural; it afforded me the opportunity to link my past experience in school cultures with the new culture that I had moved into—academia. But straddling two worlds turned out to be difficult.

Like the new staff writer who is hired to shape the stories of unfolding events that others will hear about, I was in an influential position. As I met in weekly meetings with the original planning committee, I discussed the project's form and the way in which it should be presented to school faculties. I was aware of my participation in the writing of a shared story influenced by my perspective. At times I was uncomfortable, feeling that legitimate news about an alternative way of working professionally was turning into propaganda for this alternative approach. Nevertheless, I met weekly with the original planning committee, listening to Marilyn's vision of the project and discussing the nature of collaboration and the structure of this project.

An On-Camera Roving Reporter

A strong image of our first meeting with the school faculties is still present in my memory. During this meeting it was my responsibility to explain the research component within the framework of the entire project. Like the on-camera reporter, I delivered the prepared script as viewers stared at the screen. My story held little interest for the audience. It was received with the inattention given reports of political speeches. My claims that interpretation of our data afforded opportunities to reshape the project as we proceeded drew no response.

As the project continued, my ability to participate became more complicated. While most doctoral students became university liaisons with the schools in which they already were supervising students' field experiences, I was unable to do the same because my responsibilities were with another strand of undergraduate students that I supervised in other schools. However, we decided that someone needed to coordinate the research project, and with funding from our grant we created a coordinator position that I assumed.

In this role, I saw myself peripherally connected to each of the schools. I was not a member of any one school group. Like a roving reporter, I circulated among the groups as members discussed their issues during our meetings, and I gathered information. As I stopped to listen to group discussions and offer my assistance with their school projects, I realized that I was viewed as an outsider. I was often quizzed about my presence, about my function in the project, and about what I had to offer. I encountered behavior similar to the reporter's obstacle, "No comment." As school groups struggled to establish their own trust and shared ownership of the project, my fluid, intermittent participation was disruptive. They preferred to work far from the probing reporter's eye.

Months later I discovered during an informal conversation with one group that although I was introduced as a graduate assistant, they viewed me in stereotypical terms. They thought I was an experienced university "researcher out to use [them] to get what [I] wanted without considering [their] needs." In retrospect, this incident was a critical point in my understanding of the power of positioning. I had positioned myself as a research coordinator who was available to support school efforts at the same time that the school groups positioned me as a user from the ivory tower of the academy. My role was not entirely of my own making. The participants of the project defined my role as much as I did.

A News Anchor

Following our three-hour weekly meetings with the school groups, one or two teachers from each school, identified as the "school researchers," met for an additional hour with the other researchers. During these meetings I felt like the news anchorperson, facilitating the reports from school researchers and the discussion of important issues among them. In an attempt to carry out my responsibilities in the most collaborative manner possible, I subjugated myself. Each week I started the meeting by asking, "What are we going to talk about tonight?" With these words I avoid a typical leader's control of the group agenda. This phrase became the bywords for the group—an unwritten norm of what collaboration was.

I undertook this responsibility with the belief that ongoing conversation about the attempts to work together in the schools was critical to our understanding of the nature of collaboration. I considered the teachers' doubts about their ability to do research and their reluctance to assert their views. I thought about the need to value diverse opinions and to have the direction of the conversations emerge from the group. I recognized the influence that my voice could have due to teachers' perceptions of my role. To counteract this potential impact, I decided that I should silence myself, thereby giving up the institutionalized power that was ascribed to my role, in order to create an opportunity for teachers to assume control. At the time, I believed that this action would promote a collaborative relationship between the schools and the university. But I could not always silence myself. Our discussion involved issues that I cared about and was involved in as a project participant. Trying to lead without controlling and yet participate actively in the collaborative process created intrapersonal conflict. I could not do both and maintain my romanticized conception of collaboration. Slowly I had to rethink firmly held ideas about my role, the power ascribed to it, and my interaction in a collaboration realtionship. I came to realize that I could not empower anyone. I could only monitor my voice and my actions in order to provide opportunity for others to discover their own power. I learned that power was not part of an objective reality. It was not something that I could give to other participants. Instead, I found that it was constructed in the social transactions that I had with others. Together we created the conditions in which power could emerge for individuals and for groups in varying contexts.

A New Position at a New Station

After we'd worked together for only one quarter, numerous changes occurred within our project group. Now that we had been designated a PDS, the primary focus of our project expanded to include the development of graduate students, preservice teachers, and university-based and school-based professionals. University funding for graduate associates working in the PDS meant that I could support myself while becoming a part of a school. I relished the opportunity to participate in the work with the preservice teachers, to take part in developing curricula, and to assist in planning the Quincentenary project my school was developing. This change of role was like finding a new position in broadcast journalism at a different station—a station with its own culture.

This new position placed me in the role of a new staff writer once again. As I began to work with the group in the school to which I had been assigned, I idealistically looked forward to becoming a member of the school culture. The unique nature of my institutional role, however, created an obstacle in achieving this goal. As a graduate assistant, I was a "minor" within the university. I had some rights and responsibilities, but I did not have the authority to speak on behalf of the university as I met with teachers in the project. I could only carry messages to others in positions of authority, such as Marilyn. Within the school culture I had no voice because I was an outsider. My entrée to the school was under the auspices of the collaborative project.

My most powerful memory of this new position involved the working relationship that developed. While I expected to become an integral part of our students' field experience supervision, the school's curriculum planning, and the development of the Quincentenary project, the teachers had different ideas. By assuming a large majority of the formative student-teacher supervision and by forgetting to inform me of development meetings, the teachers forced me to remain an outsider to the school culture. As with any new staff person, menial tasks, such as invitations to locate books in the library, to put papers in tote trays, to run errands to the office, and to find out the location of the week's meeting, represented my participation in the school group.

After one and a half academic quarters, a change occurred as an outgrowth of my weekly meeting with the preservice teachers. Through these meetings, I became involved in curriculum development. The interns were trying to develop instructional units and lessons for the classrooms in which they worked. As I assisted them, I indirectly assisted the classroom teachers in the school. Through my work with their student teachers, they began to value my expertise. Meaningful communication resulted. They still did not see me as a member of the culture, but occasionally they gave me an ad hoc voice within it. Through the development of relationships that obscured the parameters of an institutionally defined role, I became a collaborator and began to change positions, the way new broadcast journalists who have proved themselves do within their organizations.

20/20

As I reflected on my involvement in the project and discussed it with my PDS colleagues, I came to recognize some of the assumptions that I had carried into this collaborative experience. My attitudes were shaped by the many conversations we had before and during the project; my rethinking was provoked by my participation and the resulting frustrations and challenges to these ideas. From the beginning I believed that I had to silence my voice and limit my actions in order to give a voice to the teachers and to promote their activity. I feared that my institutional role as a graduate assistant would result in my voice becoming dominant in our conversations and my assessments carrying more weight in our supervision of preservice teachers. I tried several things. By asking, "What are we going to talk about tonight?" instead of placing anything on an agenda, by reflecting what I had heard rather than commenting on it, and by placing preservice teacher supervision in teachers' hands instead of keeping some of it in my own, I assumed that I could mitigate the influence of my role. I thought that by silencing my voice and by limiting my activity, the teachers around me would feel empowered to speak and to act.

I now see that power derived from an institutional role is not something that can be transferred to others. There is no need. It is not the power that is problematic; it is the way in which that power is used in relation to others. It can be used to oppress, or it can be used to support. To promote collaboration, it must be used to create an open forum, to create opportunity rather than to limit it.

My attempt to empower teachers caused frustration, anger, and resentment for me. Although I possessed an institutional role, the authority associated with it was at times tenuous. Sometimes my institutional role was empowering and at other times it disempowered me. Regardless, I could not empower others. I could only monitor my voice and my actions in order to provide opportunity for others to discover their own power. At all times I had to be true to myself. There could be no collaboration through self-imposed silence or inactivity.

Another assumption that I brought to the experience involved my participation in the school. Having been a teacher and a teacher advocate in the recent past, I expected that I would be embraced by the school group as a member of their culture. I thought that I would be included in informal discussions, scheduled meetings, and work sessions as an equal partner.

Upon reflection, I see the conflict between my institutional role and the role I wanted to assume. As a two-day-a-week participant, I could not become very deeply involved in the workings of the school. I was not there to share the good times and the bad. In this brief amount of time there was no way for me to understand the symbolism that the teachers used in communicating. Membership in the culture could not be offered. The most I could hope for was a developing understanding or picture of the culture.

CONCLUSION

Our focus has been the influence of our institutional roles as a university professor and a graduate associate on our collaborative relations with school-based colleagues. We entered a collaborative project with these colleagues committed to trying to work together in ways that defied the typical hierarchies of institutional roles and the power associated with them. We carried some expectations shaped by our own experience and beliefs and by the literature of collaboration. In retrospect, we see our original ideals as naive and potentially hazardous to collaboration. Our intention to give up our power as a means to establish parity did not lead us easily to collaborative modes of working together. Out of our frustrations, we were provoked into rethinking our roles in ways that allowed for more flexibility, ambiguity, and shared responsibilities. Our school colleagues helped us to understand that they did not want to be "given" power; they wanted colleagues, support, and respect. As they learned to respect their expertise, we learned the limited usefulness of our own. As they assumed new responsibilities, we learned to carry our share of the load. As they became more articulate about their beliefs, we learned how to appreciate the importance of our differences. From these collaborative insights, we are increasingly convinced that knowledge can only be partial, answers are never certain, and collaboration must be sustained by relationships rather than by romanticized requirements for collaboration determined ahead of time.

My House Is On Fire

Cynthia Tyson

Cynthia's metaphor of a house on fire calls attention to the urgency for action that many African Americans feel about the high rate of failure for students of color. This metaphor also introduces the discussion in the following chapter related to the possibility of culturally distinct modes of collaboration.

My metaphor for collaboration is a house on fire. This may seem paradoxical because collaboration seldom moves as quickly as a fire. This is my dilemma with collaboration as an African American. When I consider the dismal past and present educational legacy of African Americans in this country, I feel a tremendous sense of urgency. In educational settings, however, African Americans often work collaboratively in predominantly white and Eurocentric academic surroundings where this sense of urgency is not present. The predominant approach to collaboration operates out of an epistemology that may be in a cultural clash with more activist ways of addressing educational problems.

Let me play out my metaphor. As I take my regular route home each day, I listen to National Public Radio, which is interrupted periodically by local news bulletins. On this particular day, the bulletin is about a house fire that is now upgraded to a three-alarm fire in a local eastside neighborhood. While this is my neighborhood, I have only general thoughts about the fire and continue listening to the broadcast. A few minutes later, the newscaster announces that the major road leading to my house is open only to local traffic, due to the fire. Now my interest is piqued, but I still feel concern only about my travel.

As I approach my street, I see smoke and fire engines all over. The police have begun to block the street. I park my car and walk toward the neighborhood. As I get closer, I stop and talk to people and find out that a distant neighbor's house is on fire. I am worried because I don't want anything bad to happen to him, but I stand by patiently to see if further information is forthcoming.

Let's shift this scenario. After I park my car and walk toward the neighborhood, one of the people says that the house on fire is a brick one on the right side of the street. My heart begins to race. My house is one of the three brick ones. Further along, a person says the house is trimmed in white. My house is trimmed in white. My heart pounds faster. Then someone says the house has a fence around it—it's my house. The urgency that swells up in my heart spills over. I begin to break through the crowd, running when possible to see if my family is okay, if the pets are out, if much damage has been done. My level of urgency escalates from one of concern to one of action.

Moving from concern to action is a necessary part of collaborative efforts for African American educators. We cannot afford to sit and talk about an issue for weeks, months, and years because our educational house is on fire. The children in our neighborhoods are dropping out of school in record numbers. Collaborative talk is a beginning, but not the end. We want collaboration that leads to action and change. There is an urgency to walk the talk, not just sit and talk about the damage being done to someone else's house. It's our house that is on fire, and we want both the collaboration and the action necessary to put it out.

CHAPTER 5

African American Perspectives on Collaboration

Daa'iyah Saleem and Cynthia Tyson

In this chapter, two African American women participating in the PDS address issues of race and culture related to collaboration. Daa'iyah and Cynthia look at collaboration from a standpoint situated in particular racial and cultural practices. Their discussions challenge the practices of collaboration that emerged in this PDS. In particular, they look at issues of inclusion, equality, time, and styles of interaction. Daa'iyah, herself an MEd graduate, found that collaboration gave students a voice in decision making, but the program lacked the leadership and direction she finds in collaborative efforts in her African American communities. Cynthia and Daa'iyah then use a conversational format (reconstructed from transcripts of several tape-recorded conversations) to address several issues: the privilege associated with the time required to make collaborative decisions, the limited nature of inclusion in our model of collaboration, and the modes of interaction in the PDS, compared to those in their cultural communities.

The attention to race and culture in this chapter is not intended to deny the ways in which they are implicated throughout this book. The same acknowledgment can and should be made for issues of gender, social class, and all other orientations that mark our differences. These differences are pervasive even when unacknowledged, and they have shaped our interactions and understandings even when they were not articulated.

Minority participants in our group—university faculty, teachers/administrators, and MEd interns—have been in the minority by numbers, and their voices and perspectives, no doubt, were sometimes smothered by majority views. Racial and cultural differences have resulted in misunderstandings and misreadings of actions and intentions, some of which we have recognized and dealt with directly; at other times they are the unknown and unexamined prejudices that "hide behind our backs," to use Gadamer's (1984) metaphor. This chapter has helped us as a community to look at the cultural influences on collaboration that all of us bring to this work.

Our PDS has been committed to recruiting a culturally diverse student population, but we have been only partly successful. While we have had a larger percentage of students of color in our MEd program (10–12%) than in our undergraduate teacher education programs, our approach to collaboration may have been in conflict with the norms of collaboration in other cultures. With Cynthia and Daa'iyah's help, we are trying to understand why some of our African American students might have been uncomfortable with our attempts to work collaboratively.

Daa'iyah wrote this first section in response to my request to include her perspective in the book. As a former MEd student, she has an insider student perspective on the PDS. As part of her doctoral studies she is interested in community inclusion in education—collaboration, service learning, and parent/home involvement—which overlap with PDS collaborative goals. Her thoughts, along with the reconstructed conversation with a fellow doctoral student, Cynthia Tyson, that follows, raise issues about how we might make collaboration more culturally sensitive.

MUSINGS ON COLLABORATION AND CULTURE
Daa'iyah Saleem

Issues surrounding collaboration continually surfaced as I pursued a master's of education degree in the ECC/PDS. Collaboration took on monumental significance as my fellow MEd students and I tried to negotiate our way through an emergent certification program. My personal response to the centrality of collaboration in the program was twofold. On one hand, I enjoyed the sense of empowerment that a collaborative program fostered. There was a sense that how we, the students, felt about things really mattered. There were many times when we questioned an assignment and it was openly placed at the decision making table. Dialogue was welcomed and changes occurred.

An example of this negotiation was our case study assignment. When we began our field experience teaching in the fall, we were given the assignment of conducting a case study on a student of our choice. The assignment was due before the winter break. However, many students had problems getting the assignment completed by that time and took their concerns to the focus groups. After considerable dialogue between students, cooperating teachers, and university faculty members, the assignment and due date were adjusted. The consequence was that the assignment was more valuable to the students and it met the objectives of the faculty.

On the other hand, I had a gut-level feeling that the model of collaboration that was being used was grounded in assumptions that grow out of a specific cultural context—one I didn't share. It is very hard to generalize, of course, and I'm talking from my experiences in the African American communities of which I am a part. In these communities, collaboration seems to be the way things are done. People accept power differences, but within these differences there is a sense of equality. While there is leadership, all voices are heard. Underlying all of this is a different concept of equality.

The assumption in our PDS collaboration seems to be that all are equal players in the game, that each has an equal voice in constructing the program. This is problematic for me because "equal" is defined solely in terms of power. Equality in this model is viewed as a function of power. From my cultural viewpoint, equality is a function of intrinsic human value and a part of the balance and harmony that characterize all healthy relationships. Equality as power creates the expectation that power holders should divest themselves of their power in order to create equality. Sometimes, not always, such divestiture is not fruitful, and it may, in some cases, be dishonest. In the academy, the professors are the power brokers. Acting as if they do not have power does not remove it.

I think one of the reasons that the students in our MEd cohort were frustrated is that they were asking for less collaboration and more guidance. There was a heartfelt need to feel respected as human beings *and* to enjoy the guidance of those who were further along the path we were walking. I felt that the collaborative model being employed assumed that the best way to empower students was to ignore their requests for more structure and more predictability.

Rather than being placed alongside an array of other educational strategies, collaboration emerged as the goal displacing other goals and purposes of education. To put it more simply, collaboration became more important than educating. Now, I know it can be argued that the collaborative process is educative, and I would agree. But so are other educational processes. The goal is to select the best one for the purpose at hand and thereby maximize learning.

A RECONSTRUCTED CONVERSATION
ABOUT COLLABORATION AND CULTURE

A year after the above paper was written, Daa'iyah and another doctoral student, Cynthia Tyson, audiotaped conversations in which they discussed issues of collaboration from their culturally situated viewpoints. Cynthia is a doctoral student at the dissertation stage. At the beginning of the year she was teaching kindergarten in the Columbus public schools and working on her dissertation. The faculty person in our MEd program teaching the social studies course was assigned other responsibilities at the last moment, and Cynthia was offered an assistantship to teach the course. She resigned from her teaching position and joined the PDS, which allowed her to pursue her doctoral studies full-time.

The value of this conversation is the particular cultural perspective that both Daa'iyah and Cynthia bring to thinking about collaboration and their contrasting histories with the project. Daa'iyah is a former MEd student who followed the PDS developments closely for two subsequent years as a doctoral student in the department; Cynthia brings a newcomer's perspectives and insights. As new people often do, she helps us to continue questioning what we are doing. Cynthia's eight years of elementary classroom experience, her cultural insights, and her impressive history as resource teacher in staff development and multicultural education in Columbus public schools ground her critique and her contributions to the PDS.

CYNTHIA: I want to talk about the impact of culture on collaboration. For me, cultural specificity (or cultural relevance) is an umbrella idea that can be used to examine collaboration. As an umbrella it includes pedagogy and epistemology, as well as ethnicities and cultures as they cross and intersect with each other.

DAA'IYAH: I agree. From my experience in the PDS, one of the things that is always there but is never addressed directly is the impact of culture. We're talking about PDSs, ethnicity, culture, and the dynamics of the collaborative process.

CYNTHIA: But culture in and of itself is not the only lens that we want to use in looking at collaboration. It's part of a larger pie that needs its other parts to be whole. It's only whole when all the pieces are there. If the culture piece is missing, we don't have the whole picture.

DAA'IYAH: When the culture piece is missing, we don't have all the voices. Without asking questions about the cultural influences on collaboration, there are issues that don't get addressed. The race questions, in particular, don't get addressed.

CYNTHIA: But even when all the voices are there, it doesn't necessarily guarantee that there is equity.

DAA'IYAH: When does equity come into play?

CYNTHIA: For me, equity is about resources and privilege. Collaboration implies a give-and-take—negotiation, compromise, and sacrifice—but how does this impact on those who have the least amount to give? When we are coming to the table, some folks don't have nearly as much. Nor does everyone have the time to sit and talk through issues in an equitable way.

DAA'IYAH: Time for me is central to the issue of equity. Time is a variable of privilege. If the collaborative process takes an excessive amount of time (which it almost always does), then it tips the balance in favor of those who have the privilege of not being in a hurry. Urgency is important. It's the same urgency I think people see when they look at

African American teachers who may appear to others to be authoritarian or directive. They don't feel there is a lot of negotiating. Learning is the more immediate and central goal.

CYNTHIA: When you're sitting around the table two or three hours, for weeks, months, and in some instances, years, trying to find the best route to do something, that's privilege. In our case, we're talking about the future educators who will be educating *our* kids. We don't have the luxury of all that time. We don't have that kind of privilege because we are losing our kids every day to the streets—they are dropping out of school, they are mentally dropping out before they can physically leave. The situation is urgent.

DAA'IYAH: When I went through the PDS program, I was constantly immersed in this dialogue about collaboration, but I reached a certain level of frustration. I feel a fundamental foundation of sincerity and commitment has to be in place before you can do pretty much anything in education, and if your commitment is not to the children in the schools, then you take five hours for something that could be solved in an hour. For me, the focus needs to be getting things done for children. We have to be doing our work where it counts, not just talking about it.

CYNTHIA: In this program, it sometimes feels like the commitment is to the collaborative process and not primarily to the students in the schools.

DAA'IYAH: The urgency that different individuals bring to the table impacts on their ability to give and take in a collaborative process. Because it's our house that's on fire, I don't want to spend two and three hours talking about an issue; I really *have* to come to some closure, to make some decisions, and to see some things get done. I want to put out the fire!

CYNTHIA: In teacher education, you and I can collaborate all day long about how to do teacher preparation, but at some point, someone is going to end up in the classroom, teaching. I am trying to think of my own community and growing up. Again, it's a different sense of urgency. I remember at one point the church, the school, and the parents decided there was going to be a block watch, and then everybody met and talked about it. The church, the school, the parents, the police department all met to collaborate and to make a plan. The ultimate goal was better neighborhood security. Once the planning ended and the implementation began, the collaboration continued, but a plan of action was carried out.

DAA'IYAH: The implementation can begin and the collaboration continues because there is a central consensus about the goal. Collaboration is not the goal but the process. It doesn't have to go on and on before something can get done.

CYNTHIA: Most people of color use collaboration as a tool, because it takes more than just themselves to address community problems. It makes me think of the African proverb "I am because we are."

DAA'IYAH: I have another issue to bring up. In my experience in the PDS, there was also something in the feel and fiber of the program itself that wasn't welcoming. In my MEd cohort, we started off with four African Americans—one was African Latino—but I was the only one who finished the program. While people did have some clear reasons for dropping out (getting married, changing careers), it may also have been related to how the program felt. Often I felt like I was swimming upstream, despite the fact that it was a collaborative model. When you have a clear imbalance in terms of those with different ethnicities and cultural backgrounds, you have to find a way to have everybody's voice heard and valued.

CYNTHIA: We assume that collaboration means that it is inclusive and inviting, but it's not, even when people are trying.

DAA'IYAH: I think people were trying, and with the best intentions. However, good intentions don't necessarily mean culturally sensitive results.

CYNTHIA: In my example, the community was what made the collaboration work.

DAA'IYAH: But community is not a given. It can't be taken for granted.

CYNTHIA: I think that the kinds of things that make for successful collaboration, however, are too often treated as givens.

DAA'IYAH: There are specific and culturally based things that happen in the African American community that support the interactions that build community. In particular, there is a general attentiveness to the humanness of relationships and the importance of connections between people.

CYNTHIA: There are ways of doing business in cultural contexts that support those connections. I often feel like the personal connections are missing in other cultural settings. For example, in a PDS meeting recently, two folks came in to discuss some ideas they had for a project. The meeting began, and they started to describe their project. That went on for forty minutes, and then they asked for questions. My first question was, "Who are these people at this meeting?" The person leading the meeting said, "I've done it again." He had not introduced those attending the meeting. Culturally, in an African American community, I can't imagine that would have happened. It's the same in feminist communities. It is very important that people deal with connecting people to their lives. Their life experience makes the situation richer.

DAA'IYAH: I think one of the key things that is not dealt with in collaboration is a sense of self. In terms of the university, first you have to start reaching people on a human level. This comes back to the community. If nobody knows what you're about, and then they try to talk with you, the input they get will be different than if you are with a circle of your friends.

CYNTHIA: There have been very few times in this program when someone has asked me how I am doing in my doctoral program. Even people with whom I have been sitting around the collaborative table since the fall, they don't even know what my research is about. The woman who checks my groceries at my neighborhood grocery store can tell you what I am researching, because every time she sees me she asks me how it's going. The maintenance worker who picks up trash around my apartment knows, the kids who live in my apartment complex do. I don't think we can collaborate without supporting each other. There are clearly some cultural differences here.

DAA'IYAH: We talk about building community with the students. I don't know if the folks who are trying to create that for the PDS students have created it for themselves. That is something that we can learn together, but the difference is that we all go about doing that differently based on our culture, ethnicity, and social class.

DAA'IYAH: So what does collaboration mean when you pull a bunch of people together who don't have the same cultural backgrounds, who don't relate to others in the same way, who don't define collaboration in the same way?

CYNTHIA: When you don't give attention to those relational things, a collaborative process doesn't serve everyone well because inevitably the process and the goals are different.

DAA'IYAH: I think that many people are comfortable with this model because they are comfortable with the silences, comfortable with not having everyone at the table. There is an unrecognized exclusion of people who are central to the educative process, and yet people think they are collaborating.

CYNTHIA: To collaborate in isolation is oxymoronic.

DAA'IYAH: Collaboration implies inclusion.

CYNTHIA: I think this is where culture comes into play. Being a part of a relational culture means that you can't leave those folks out. I would never think I could go into the community and plan something for kids in that community without talking to the parents, finding out what is going on in the larger community, and finding out what folks want to do and don't want to do. Then we could try together to create a program to help children, parents, teachers, and the community at large.

DAA'IYAH: My experience is that much of the collaboration in the African American community has this built-in sense of inclusion.

CYNTHIA: Teacher education programs historically have been isolated at the university level. Closer work with the schools is supposed to make them more collaborative and inclusionary, but not all the stakeholders are included. If it were truly inclusive, teachers, parents, students, and the community at large would be at the table. Teacher education has to be more inclusive than just the schools and university working together.

DAA'IYAH: What you are doing is critiquing the models of collaboration that are out there and saying that many are not fully collaborative. From my perspective, if you want collaboration, collaboration implies inclusion.

CYNTHIA: There are ethical requirements for collaboration, but there are also practical ones. It's like planning a wedding and being stuck with the constraints of your finances, traditionally the finances of the bride's father. If you bring the groom's family into the finances, then the same constraints are no longer there.

DAA'IYAH: There are probably many reasons why collaboration in teacher education is not as inclusive as it should be. Even when people try to use feel good approaches like collaboration, there are so many unnamed and obscured nuances that are in the racist fibers of society that it makes people from other cultures uncomfortable. I think you find people of color turning away from circles where this kind of collaboration is the norm.

CYNTHIA: But are we arguing that collaboration is not a good model for teacher education or for this program?

DAA'IYAH: No, I don't think collaboration in general is wrong. I think what they need in this program is in place, but the cultural piece is missing. We talk about how it takes a village to raise a child. If you really believe that, then everybody who is a stakeholder has to be at the table.

CYNTHIA: As we talk, it's really clear to me how deep these issues are.

DAA'IYAH: They are deep, but I wonder if collaboration as a model, even though it is entrenched in a racist society, provides a more workable context for creating change. Can we use this model to address issues of racism, inclusion, and equity in education more easily than in other organizational arrangements?

CYNTHIA: In theory, a collaborative model is inclusive and also responsive to critique. In practice, I hope that this critique will include a fundamental examination of its embeddedness in a racist society.

Making Muffins From Scratch

Marilyn Johnston

The metaphors in these interludes either originated in or were extended by group conversation. In one conversation where we were brainstorming, a weekly event at my house—making muffins—developed into a metaphor for the open-endedness of our PDS development. Using this metaphor has forced me to think harder about the extent to which the development of innovative practices is truly open-ended, as well as about the inescapable influence of our experience on our understandings.

My husband makes muffins each weekend to take in his lunches. He has two requirements—that they're healthy, and that their construction serve a useful purpose. He likes to put bran, yeast, nuts, and lots of grains in them to make them healthy. He also likes to use things up from the garden or the leftovers in the refrigerator. No standard recipe can meet the requirements of the changing ingredients and standards of healthiness he requires, so he makes them up from scratch each time. Sometimes they're delicious; sometimes they're not. There are jokes around the house about who will be the guinea pig each week to test their suitability for eating. Of course, he doesn't care much about our evaluation. I think he secretly hopes the rest of the household won't like them so he'll have more for himself.

Maybe the PDS is like Mike cooking without a recipe. We started with some sense of what is required for a PDS and some interests in a particular form of collaboration, and yet we weren't sure how putting this diverse set of people and ideas together was going to work out. With all these unknowns, we couldn't predict its success.

In the summer of 1994, we organized some open discussion groups, called Coffee and Conversations. In one of these conversations, talking about my metaphor (a small part of it is presented below) helped me to develop my ideas further.

HELEN: So, just throw it all in and see what happens. (laughter)
MARILYN: We've been throwing a lot of things into our PDS, but we're still not sure of what we've got.

JOAN: To make muffins hold together, you have to *use certain ingredients*.
MARILYN: Even so, sometimes they don't hold together and sometimes they
    come out hard to chew.
BETH: What do you do if the recipe doesn't turn out right?
MARILYN: Mike always eats his muffins.
TIM: Amazing.
HELEN: But what is a good muffin? Does a good muffin *depend on taste or
    healthiness?*
MARILYN: Taste is not a primary criterion for Mike. It's whether they're
    healthy and whether they've used good ingredients.
JOAN: I'd like to know what goes in some of those muffins.

It was only when I studied this transcript later that I realized the provocative ideas it contained. The comment about using certain ingredients made
me rethink both the muffins and our PDS. My husband's comments went in
the same direction. He does not see his muffins as unique. Muffins always
require flour, shortening, eggs, and liquid in somewhat regular proportions.
For him, the added ingredients make them a little unusual, but not unique.
You may not often see zucchini-and-raspberry or rhubarb-and-rice muffins in
the store, yet they are not that different in basic ways from "regular" muffins,
if the basic ingredients are considered.

The ways in which social knowledge guides our PDS development may
well be of a similar kind. In our context, many things we are doing feel new.
We are creating a collaborative culture where none existed before. Yet school/
university collaboration is not a new idea, and we have not made up on our
own the ideas that guide our work. The ideas we absorb from reading and
talking to others steep our discourse and ways of talking to each other. The
political context in general supports collaborative work, school districts are
moving to site-based management approaches, and universities across the
country are responding to critiques of teacher education by working more
closely with schools. Seen from this social context, the PDS loses a sense of
making it up from scratch, just as Mike's muffins now seem less unique to me
than they once did.

The question whether *good muffins depend on taste or healthiness* is
provocative. At first I tried to pull these two apart: there are reasons to choose
taste, and reasons to choose healthiness. Mike's response was to ask why these
were choices. From his perspective, his muffins both taste good and are
healthy. From my perspective, they sometimes taste good and sometimes not.
Maybe taste is an aspect of personal preference, while healthiness is a more
objective criterion. How much do PDSs depend on personal taste? Clearly,
some people have not stayed with us because collaboration was not attractive. They found the process too ambiguous, the commitment too time con-

suming, or the critical reflection too threatening. The healthiness of a muffin seems less controversial. Ingredients can be identified and their health potential calculated. Can we argue for the healthiness of a PDS in the same way? Do we have professional agreement that collaboration between schools and universities is the best way to reform teacher education and promote professional development, inquiry, and change? If my own college is a reasonable sample, I would have to say no. Many of my colleagues think that collaboration is not worth the time and money it requires and that it detracts from the scholarly agenda of the university. We may be able to argue for the worth of this endeavor, but many do not want to partake. How do we tell when we have a good muffin? How do we know when we have a good PDS?

CHAPTER 6

School-Based Voices and Stories

Kathleen Iböm

In this chapter, school-based participants write about their participation in the PDS. Their stories cover a wide range of interests and experiences, and their voices reflect their situated views of our collaborative experience. Charlene Williams, a school counselor, writes about the difficulties of understanding the PDS and its goals from the perspective of a new participant. Kathleen Iböm, a clinical educator, puzzles about why teachers are treated differently than other professionals with regard to professional development opportunities and how the PDS is different in this respect. Sue Wightman, who has supervised many student teachers, including four MEd interns, reflects on writing an interactive journal with one of her interns. Her reflections help her to think about the value of collaboration. Don Cramer, in an interview with Marilyn, talks about what he has learned about collaboration as a PDS school principal. Lisa Westhoven, clinical educator and co-coordinator of the PDS, shares her classroom with a partner teacher, Katie Barnes, a former intern in the PDS program. Together they write about the advantages and challenges of their shared teaching, which extends collaboration from the PDS into their classroom.

UNEXPECTED OUTCOMES
Charlene Williams

My colleague, Melba Bias, urged me to get involved in the PDS program when I was looking for a course to take at the university. She said it would be beneficial for me and for the school. Melba talked with such great excitement about the PDS program that I agreed to participate for the next quarter. Little did I realize that I was about to embark on a *real* learning experience.

When I walked into the first Thursday meeting, I did not know what was going on. There was a lot of talking and discussing. I listened intently because I felt confused about what was happening. I thought that maybe I was missing something, because everyone else seemed to understand what was going on. I quietly asked my school colleagues seated nearby to explain what was happening. I said that I felt as though I had "just walked in on the middle of a movie." They chuckled, yet they assured me that all was well and that this was how the meetings functioned. After a while, they assured me, I would feel more comfortable.

I was not certain about that because this class was not similar to any class I had ever taken at the university. It seemed there was no structure to the meeting. I read the chapters that were assigned, I went to the class, and I conferenced with my school colleagues, but I continued to feel uncomfortable and confused. I wondered to myself, "What did I allow Melba to get me into?"

Then, on May 11, everything began to make sense. During the class we watched a group do a practice presentation for a conference they were going to the following day. The presentation was about the PDS and what individuals had learned from their experience. Everything became crystal clear as I discovered there was a "method to this madness." I began to understand that the true purpose of the class was to foster self-development.

I realized later why it was so difficult for me to adjust to this PDS approach to learning. All of my education and teaching experience so far had been carried out in the traditional mode. I was told what was expected, and I conformed and performed accordingly. There was no true dialogue. The professional development courses that I had taken previously gave me information but offered no real opportunities to share what I had learned professionally with my colleagues.

I have been teaching for 30 years. Here I am at the end of my career, getting involved in a project that is helping me understand what collaboration and professional development is all about.

AFTER HOURS
Kathleen Ibóm

Other occupations recognize the importance of growth in one's profession. Lawyers practice law in front of the judge and jury part of the time. The rest of their time is left to research and preparation. Their performance is then judged by others in the courtroom, and they grow from watching and learning from each other.

Doctors are always learning about new procedures and meeting with their colleagues to share knowledge and technology. My dentist explained to me that he schedules around 25 hours for patients, the other 20 for research and consultations with other dentists.

Many businessmen spend a minimal amount of time with their clients. The bulk of their time is spent trying to find ways to improve and present their products. Even university professors are given a limited number of hours of time teaching. The rest is dedicated to preparation and research.

Why are classroom teachers expected to spend the bulk of their day teaching 25 to 35 children? No value is given to research, reflection, and preparation. All of the above are expected to be taken care of "after hours." How can we get better at our work if we are not given time—time to share and reflect?

The PDS has helped me make the time and given me the network necessary for growth.

REFLECTIONS OF A COLLABORATING TEACHER
Sue Wightman

Early this school year, I had the opportunity to reread a shared journal that my year-long intern and I kept together. It reminded me that thinking and reflecting are central to the teaching and learning process. Among the pages, the word *change* appears again and again. I was struck with how many changes occurred within that year for the intern and for myself. What was it, I wondered, that made that year so free and easy? What is it about teaching that stimulates renewal? Why is reflecting about teaching practice such an important part of the professional package? How do collaborating teachers transmit excitement to an intern preoccupied with "getting things right"? When does commitment turn into an expressive art? Where does the artist-teacher go for new ideas?

I found that some of the answers to these questions were lurking in the pages of the shared journal. I found that looking back through a beginning teacher's eyes helped me begin to rethink this thing called teaching.

The beginning of our shared journal can be characterized as preliminary groundwork—the intern and I exchanged some basic information about our lives and our theories of education. He was convinced that teaching was the greatest job anyone could ever have. I was convinced that it was the most complicated! He wanted "to do everything exactly" as I did, stating that the "fire that drove me" was contagious and illuminating for him. I was concerned that the fire was banked and smoldering. He wrote pages about his plans for the future. I wrote about plans gone awry and the benefits of leaving a little room for life to unfold. He talked about "really communicating with the kids," and I added my agreement.

Back and forth we wrote as the year progressed, seeking immediate answers to the classroom management problems inherent in a kindergarten and puzzling over how I did things in "such an effortless way." Somewhere around February, the journal took a specific turn toward dissecting that "effortless" manner, and for the first time in a long time I was forced to examine how I created the learning environment. The important word here is *create*—to make something new, to originate, to instigate, to bring into being. Much in the way the artist approaches the blank canvas, the sculptor circles the stone, and the writer agonizes over capturing just the right feeling with words, teaching is grounded in the ability to bring ideas into being.

Once we had pinned down our definitions of *create*, we began to list examples in our practice that showed it. The journal entries got longer and more complicated. He wrote about the difficulty he was having getting all the children to participate in a whole group activity. I encouraged him to try an outrageous way of engaging them. He rose to the occasion and invented a game that required cooperation. He told the children that one of them would be a mother sheep (we were in the middle of an animal unit) and another would be the lamb. Still other children would be partner wolves, mother, and cub. The object, he said, was to show how mothers try to provide for and protect their young. As the game began, the wolves departed over the hill to lie in wait while the sheep and lambs mingled on the green. As the wolves approached, the sheep enclosed their young in a circle, protecting them. The wolves sought out lambs who were left unattended. Alas, those were "eaten." The children played this game for weeks, wrote stories about survival and strength in numbers, and produced highly detailed drawings of the game process. The way the intern looked, the way he spoke to the children, and the way he sat, replete, at the end of the day was the perfect illustration of creating. He had had a heady taste of the freedom that goes along with the ability to create.

Within the pages of our journal are many examples of incidents of freedom. I am convinced that the act of creating in the classroom can take many forms. It is stirring to see a teacher in the process of perfecting his or her art. It is even more rewarding when children accept their role in the creation of their own education. The process will look different for every teacher and every learner. By its very nature, however, the act of learning is creating something new and valuable to the artist. We can play with the elements of teaching. We can prescribe curriculum and theory. We can examine what works and what doesn't. But in the final analysis, teaching and learning are much more than elements, issues, and investigations. The teacher who is an artist taps into freedom and finds the joy of creating. It has an unforgettable taste.

CONVERSATION WITH A PRINCIPAL
Don Cramer and Marilyn Johnston

MARILYN: Don, you were the principal of the first school to join the Quincentenary project. You were also the only principal to attend our Thursday meetings on a regular basis. For three years as a principal you were also the administrative representative on the co-coordinator team that oversaw the thirteen PDS projects at the university. Since you retired last year, you have taken on new responsibilities coordinating the school/university partnerships at Ohio State and are wearing a new hat. But as you think back over your experience as a principal, what did you learn about collaboration?

DON: Collaboration with the university made me more aware of how I was working and interacting with my staff. Collaboration was not a big administrative style change for me, because I think I was always quite collaborative or sought help from teachers, but it did change how I talked about it. When we talk about collaboration in an explicit way, it makes people feel like they are part of the process. Collaboration legitimatizes teachers' roles in decision making and makes their participation explicit and important. Collaboration also brings out leadership qualities in people who maybe weren't participating fully before.

MARILYN: How does that work?

DON: Talking about participation explicitly means that someone affirms that it's okay for everyone to put in their two cents.

MARILYN: It legitimates the process of working together?

DON: Right. When you start talking about collaboration, it makes the process of how we're working together come to the surface, whereas before it was just swirling around, mostly unnoticed. Another thing it does is to evaluate those who have been the leaders. If they were hogging the stage, it makes them look in the mirror and ask, "Am I really being collaborative?"

MARILYN: In the beginning you had a staff of mostly experienced teachers. They expected a certain kind of leadership from you, even though they were strong individual themselves.

DON: I think traditionally teachers expect leadership because that's how schools are organized. They want to be able to say to a parent or a student, "Mr. Cramer wants it *this way*." They also want a principal to take care of problems and support them when parents have complaints. They want to be free to do their job.

MARILYN: Is this leadership role incompatible with collaboration?

DON: I think it provides an opportunity or stage for shared leadership. It allows others to assist in the leadership role.

MARILYN: How is collaboration connected with professional development?

DON: I think that most teachers are interested in professional development. By and large, they've not been given many real opportunities. They do summer workshops or things after school. Most teachers, however, feel like they've been pounded into the ground with after-school staff development that doesn't come to much. Collaboration with the university has allowed us to talk differently.

MARILYN: What do you mean?

DON: School districts are notorious for telling teachers what they need, whether they want it or not. Some teachers like that. Collaboration is a way of talking more openly about what we can do in our own school settings to make it better. The collaborative part of the discussion gives people license to talk freely, for everyone to be an equal part of the conversation. We haven't really done this before. It's been the principal or inservice committee's job to set up the inservice for their school. Collaboration has opened the door to this discussion. Everyone is brought into the process—the bus drivers, the secretary, the custodians. Everyone is a part of making the school community a better place and giving it direction.

MARILYN: That's because the collaborative approach values everyone's voice?

DON: If it's autocratic, the person who hasn't said anything for years is never going to speak up. They come to the meeting and go home and complain about it, but if we have a collaborative community, then everyone has a piece of the action. Everyone is a part of planning the professional development. When we planned PDS things to do in the summer, everyone was there. We paid everyone the same from our grant monies—everyone who is involved in the life of the school. In this process, it is essential to create a focus and then it takes funds to support it. In the end, of course, something has to happen. It can't be business as usual. You have to see that you're getting something out of the process which is ownership. Of course, the process is more difficult and more complicated because more people are putting in ideas. It's more difficult to get a decision made and carry though on things. It's hard work! Some people are more comfortable with an autocratic approach because they don't want to take the time, or, even more important, they don't want to have the responsibility for making it work.

MARILYN: Is that to say schools in general are not very collaborative?

DON: They probably aren't. I think there is movement in the collaborative direction, but we haven't gotten there yet. Schools are pretty much like they were fifty to a hundred years ago. We haven't changed the organization of schools. We haven't even changed the physical arrangement and appearance of schools much. We still often have twenty-five little desks and one big desk facing each other.

MARILYN: What do you think it takes to make schools more collaborative?

DON: I think it boils down to trust. I think it also depends on what you want out of school. The more a school takes on complex issues, the more I think the principal needs to be collaborative. If you want to have plain old school, one person can do it. The traditional role of the principal works in these cases. But if you start reaching out, like we did with partnerships with the university—a Discipline-Based Art Education program, looking at social issues, bringing parents into the school, adopt-a-school business partners, etc.—one person can't do all this. You have to have collaborative structures to support all these activities and make them work.

MARILYN: So why don't more principals work collaboratively?

DON: I think the biggest issue has to do with the system—it's about how the system views collaboration and collaborative decision making. For example, in the Columbus school district right now, principals are worried about their schools being closed and people losing their jobs. This affects how people go about business. If you're in a position where you might be fired, collaborative decision making is dangerous.

MARILYN: Why?

DON: Principals feel that they need to be in control of things. If everything falls apart, it's the principal's fault. The principal is going to be viewed as having or not having strong leadership skills by the way the school operates and is perceived by others.

MARILYN: So job security pushes principals toward more controlling leadership styles?

DON: Sure, collaboration feels risky and open ended when your job is on the line.

MARILYN: But aren't school districts advocating site-based management and community involvement?

DON: Yes, but if the ship is going down, the principal's to blame. Collaboration and job insecurity don't mix together easily when there are problems. You can say that you're doing all these collaborative things, but if things go to hell in a handbasket, then you're the one who caused the failure. A climate of trust has to be established in the whole system if there's going to be collaboration.

MARILYN: What's the university's role in this?

DON: I don't think that the university really understands the politics of the schools and the school systems and how the central office and supervisory responsibilities influence principals. They don't really appreciate the power of parents, either. Vocal parents exert an enormous influence on the stability of a school.

MARILYN: So the university comes out and says let's do all this collaboration without being sensitive to how it affects principals' lives?

DON: The intentions are good, but they have little idea of how it's going to affect the principal's position in the district, or how it will affect children and parents in the school. Failure due to risk taking can be long lasting.

MARILYN: The fact is that collaboration can put principals in jeopardy?

DON: Right. That's why principals, a lot of them, shy away from getting involved with the university and their collaborative efforts.

MARILYN: It sounds like collaboration means they have to respond to two different sets of expectations.

DON: The principal already has the expectations of parents, teachers, and the central office. The expectations from the central office are to keep everyone happy. You have school board members who are elected, and you have superintendents who are renewed every two years, and they want people to be happy.

MARILYN: But they also want innovation and reform.

DON: Sure, the school board wants to hear that we're on the cutting edge of education. But they want you to get it done without any discomfort or problems. That easy—just make sure everyone is happy while you're doing all these reform initiatives. That's really counter to what it's all about. You have to dig up the ground to make something grow. When you dig up the ground, it gets dirty and muddy.

MARILYN: So how does the university fit into the reform picture?

DON: The university is pushing for collaboration, for teacher education reform, for new ways of teaching, which may or may not be in line with what the school district is supporting. The principal has to make it all fit together.

MARILYN: So how did you do that?

DON: We were able to make the PDS and school reform into a plus rather than a liability. I talked to the parents about how the PDS provided additional resources for their kids. It made the parents proud that their kids were a part of this special school. It made the staff feel like they were being recognized. And we could say to the central office that we had been selected by the university to be a teaching laboratory. If we were going to be a part of these different agendas, I had to make sure that people understood them. You can't just ignore the parents, or the district office, when you're developing these partnerships. I was talking to a new PDS principal and she was concerned about her parents being upset with all these people around the school. We talked about how she could talk with the parents to help them recognize that these people were bringing in extra resources for their kids. You have to bring these separate agendas together in a positive way.

MARILYN: Sounds like a lot of PR work with parents, the school district, and the university.

DON: Right, it's very political. You have two systems you're working with that really don't understand each other. The principal is caught in the middle and it's sometimes very uncomfortable, yet it can be very productive.

MARILYN: This increases the complexity and the political nature of your job, right? You used to have to play politics in the school district, and now you have to do that at the university as well.

DON: Yes, but at the same time it allows you to do things that you probably wouldn't be allowed to do otherwise. I was able to get substitutes and get people released to do things because I had this license as a PDS to do things differently. I don't think the school system understood what I was doing at all, but I could say, "This is PDS and school reform." We [speaking from my role as partnership coordinator at the university] do the same thing at the university. We get to do things because we're partnered with the schools that we wouldn't get to do otherwise. The faculty sometimes don't understand what's happening, either, but we just say this is PDS and reform. It's complex, but if you take advantage of it, it can work to the advantage of your individual school and the university. A lot of it has to do with neither institution knowing what you're doing. It's a bit like chaos theory.

MARILYN: What other challenges does collaboration create?

DON: Schools are very self-protecting places. When you start to talk about what goes on in school with folks who are outside the school, it creates a whole new set of challenges.

MARILYN: How?

DON: Collaboration exposes some of the fragile relationships that exist in schools. This is a real roadblock to developing partnerships. You have to be quite confident as a school staff and principal to open yourself up for this kind of scrutiny, to do what Ken Howey and Nancy Zimpher (1989) call "defending your practice." It's hard for somebody who's been teaching for twenty years to say, "I really screwed up and here's what I should have done." Collaboration fills in the moat that has traditionally protected schools from outsiders.

MARILYN: But there have been moats around individual classroom as well, right?

DON: Definitely. Teachers traditionally have not talked to each other about their professional practice. During one of our staff meetings we walked around to each other's rooms and people talked about what they were doing. There were teachers in the building who had never been in their colleagues' classrooms, even though they had taught there for ten or fifteen years.

MARILYN: What was your motivation for doing that?

DON: I thought there were a lot of great ideas in the school. I wanted teachers to get to know each other better, to be able to share ideas, to be more collaborative. You know, in the medical profession, doctors share ideas and compare notes. However, for teachers, sharing puts them in an awkward position; it's almost like you're considered a show-off if you've found a better way to teach fractions. So we came up with the idea to use a staff meeting and walk around the school. It got a lot of teachers sharing ideas and questioning their practice.

MARILYN: I've heard this called "reculturing" the school.

DON: For people to work in the same place and not know what each other is doing does seem ridiculous. And yet some teachers are comfortable with this.

MARILYN: They are threatened by the prospect of scrutiny?

DON: Collaboration puts professionals in a different relationship with each other. Through our collaboration we learn about what's going on in the school and at the university. Sometimes it's not a pretty picture. Problems that are created from exposure add fuel to the fire for those people who don't want to do it anyway. It gives them ammunition to say, "If we didn't have this partnership going on, no one would have known about the problem." Administrators don't need that kind of trouble.

MARILYN: It makes the dirty laundry public.

DON: Very much so, and of course, you have university faculty, interns, or principals who don't know how to handle the problems, or don't do it in a sensitive way. Someone's teaching gets talked about in a class at the university, and all hell breaks loose. It takes a lot of skill to handle school/university partnerships.

MARILYN: Given all these challenges, who does this collaboration?

DON: If you really want to do something for the profession, it's an opportunity. I don't know whether I would have been willing to jump into something like this as a newer principal. At that point I had other concerns—hours, job security, children's education, etc.

MARILYN: So what's the outcome of all of this?

DON: There are so many agendas that the principal has to deal with. To work collaboratively, you have to have someone help you learn what it's all about. I don't think it just happens. The dramatic changes in our school and with many of the teachers would not have happened without the connection we've had with OSU.

MARILYN: Neither would the university have been able to make some of the
changes that we've made without your input. Our collaboration has
clearly influenced both institutions.

COLLABORATIVE TEACHING: A VEHICLE FOR CHANGE
Mary Kathleen Barnes and Lisa Westhoven

There are many forms of collaboration in our PDS. Our shared teaching
of a single classroom is one of them. Lisa is one of the co-coordinators and a
clinical educator in our PDS. She teaches our third-grade classroom in the
morning and does PDS work in the afternoon. Katie is her teaching partner.
Katie is a former graduate of the MEd program and teaches half-time with Lisa
while also doing a doctoral program at Ohio State University. We are in our
third year of teaching together. Our collaborative teaching allows both of us
time to participate in other professional development activities.

A collaborative teaching partnership was a relatively new concept in our
district, so we spent considerable time thinking about how to communicate
effectively to parents. We wanted them to understand how our teaching partnership would work. Lisa had another partner for part of the previous school
year. Some parents reacted negatively to this change, and we wanted to address parental concerns prior to the start of the school year.

We briefly explained our arrangement to parents during the open house,
the night before school started. Two weeks after school began, the curriculum night gave us an opportunity to explain our shared teaching responsibilities and professional development activities. We discussed our vision for this
school year and provided specific information about how the classroom would
operate and our expectations for our students. We explained that as a result
of Lisa's participation in the university's PDS initiative, she would be able to
enrich our students' classroom experience with visits from university professors and educators from around the world. Lisa also had a teacher education
student from the MEd program who would be spending the first 10 weeks of
the year in our classroom, thus providing further enrichment and more individual attention for our students. Katie would bring the new ideas she was
learning in graduate school.

As expected, we received a variety of reactions. Some parents were concerned about placing their child in what they perceived to be an experimental classroom, others raised questions about the continuity and consistency
of having two teachers, others worried about communication, and still others wondered about expectations and teaching styles. Some parents were
excited at the prospect of having two perspectives on their child's growth

and development, other parents commented that more resources would be brought into the classroom with two teachers.

Although we never formally described our partnership to the staff, we got informal feedback from some staff members. Several teachers referred to Lisa's half day at the university as her "time off." One teacher even asked if she went shopping during that time. Some teachers felt that committed teachers wouldn't leave their classes every day. Our various principals have all assumed that we were two full-time teachers each carrying full responsibilities for duties and committee work. The staff rarely expected us to perform half-time responsibilities. Even though Katie was expected to do her full share of responsibility, she struggled for equal status. It took three years before she got her own mailbox. It took many reminders that we needed paperwork to come with both our names on it. It has taken considerable effort to help others understand our arrangement.

We see many benefits to our collaborative teaching partnership. Perhaps the most significant is the benefit of having two perspectives for each child. Each of us considers each child's strengths and weaknesses, and we share these perspectives with each other. This sharing has allowed us to identify students with special needs and begin intervention quite early in the school year.

Some students who have behavior problems are able to get a "fresh start" each day after lunchtime with the "new" teacher. This was an unexpected benefit, but we believe it is particularly significant. Many of these children require a great deal of attention and their varied demands are more easily met when they can be shared by two individuals.

The risk of burnout is also greatly reduced because we can share the load, and our experiences, and laugh and commiserate about our achievements and disappointments. Although many teachers share war stories in the faculty lunchroom, we can collaborate on an entirely different level because we are closely involved with the same group of children.

Our collaboration has also improved our communication with parents. We can discuss parental expectations together and share our perceptions about the best ways to meet them. The support of another teacher is invaluable in those occasional "difficult" conferences. We are keenly aware, however, of possible intimidation when two teachers are present at parent conferences. We structure our conferences very informally in order to ensure that parents feel comfortable.

Another unexpected outcome is the additional time devoted to planning and reflection. We spend more time planning than a single teacher typically does. We do individual planning and reflecting, and then we spend time talking with each other. We discuss at length what we are doing and why. This is a different process than planning alone. By sharing our planning, we are more thoughtful and focused, and therefore our teaching is more effective. With our energies focused on integrating three or four content areas for our half day, instead of seven or eight for the full day, we spend more time finding resources and developing activities.

A special collegiality can develop in this kind of collaborative teaching that is different than working with other teachers even at the same grade level. When we talk, we discuss the same children within the same context and environment. We are able to think more deeply about each student, and as a result, we can better meet each student's needs. At times we see things differently, and this helps us to begin to reshape or rethink our practice. We feel free to question each other's assumptions, and this pushes us each to think about our practices in new ways. Sometimes this reflection reaffirms our beliefs, and at other times it shapes new perspectives.

Our teaching partnership allows each of us to take advantage of professional development opportunities, and our students rarely need a substitute teacher. The benefits of this are twofold. First, most teachers complain about the time it takes to prepare for a substitute. After attending professional activities, many teachers wearily complain that it's not worth all the trouble. This is not a problem for us. We are each familiar with what the other is doing in class, and if one of us needs to be away, it is merely a matter of a phone call and a quick review of the plans. We don't have to worry about a day that is lost to "busy work" in order to keep the kids occupied and well behaved for the substitute.

We also get twice the mileage out of our professional development hours because we share with each other what we have learned and the implications that it might have for our students. Our experience has been that there is little time allotted for processing and discussion during most professional development workshops. In our collaborative teaching partnership, we have the opportunity to process what we have learned.

There are, of course, problems in our collaborative teaching arrangement. The most significant is time. It is faster and more convenient to develop teaching units and plans on your own, without having to coordinate everything. Report card time is also time consuming, as we carefully discuss our evaluations of each student and develop the narrative part of the progress report together.

Communication may also be more difficult with other members of the faculty or school personnel. For example, Lisa's university schedule occasionally conflicts with our school grade-level meetings, so she is sometimes dependent upon Katie to share information with her. Katie's university course schedules occasionally conflict with faculty meetings, so she is dependent upon Lisa for information. Again, we need to spend additional time to recap the meetings for each other.

Another difficulty is the shortage of space in the classroom. While we were able to make space for two desks, finding storage space for two teachers' materials has been impossible. Katie stores most of her materials at home.

It is difficult in a partnership to ensure that parents communicate with the correct teacher regarding specific assignments. Occasionally a parent will ask a teacher about specific assignments in a content area for which she is not responsible. This has potential for creating two problems—parents do not get the information they need at the time of their initial inquiry, and parents may perceive this as a lack of communication between us.

We share many basic beliefs and attitudes toward teaching. But there are also differences in personalities, work styles, management styles, and sometimes goals. These have to be discussed and negotiated in ways that do not damage the trust and care we have built together. Again, it takes time to attend to our differences and work out mutually supportive ways of dealing with and learning from them.

In conclusion, we believe that schools need a new vision for the role of school-based educators. Based on our experience, we argue that collaborative teaching partnerships have the potential to play a significant role in advancing education toward this new vision. Collaborative teaching has the potential both to improve teaching and promote ongoing professional development.

Learning to Ride a Bike

Lisa Westhoven

Explaining our PDS to others is difficult. In particular, how we are organized and how the schools and universities work together is complicated. Lisa Westhoven, a clinical educator/co-coordinator of the PDS and third-grade teacher, has used the metaphor of a bicycle to explain school/university collaboration, and learning to ride a bike as analogous to learning about collaboration.

Our PDS works between The Ohio State University and local schools. These two components can be compared to the front and the back wheels of a bike. Each part can function independently of the other, and for years there has been little that connected the two. They operated more as two unicycles than as a bicycle. As a result of this arrangement, influencing one another has been accidental at best. Each has had its own way of working and was not dependent on the other. Put together as a bicycle, there is interaction and connection.

The chains and gears make the front and back wheels work together. Likewise, the PDS is the mechanism through which the schools and university can begin to work together collaboratively. The gears, chains, and wheels must all work together in order to go somewhere. Likewise, our schools and the university must work together if collaboration is going to succeed.

I used this metaphor the first time to explain the PDS to a new principal in my building. He wanted to know who was the leader if neither institution "owned" the PDS. I explain that leadership was changeable, like riders of a bike who take turns. In the PDS, we have different roles—professors, teachers, co-teachers, clinical educators, principals, and graduate associates. Each of these roles brings a needed perspective to teacher education and professional development and each takes its turn providing leadership. Many participants actually take on multiple roles. For example, I am a classroom teacher, a co-coordinator of the PDS, a co-teacher of a social studies methods course, and a clinical educator. Other participants provide direction through contributing to conversations, asking questions, and participating in decision making.

It takes a lot of energy to pedal a PDS. One person cannot do all the leading. At times, directions are shouted from participants who understand how the bike works. At any time a rider may get off the bike and another rider may get on. The new rider may step on the brakes or turn in a new direction. Of course, without the support of the group (like training wheels), pedaling may be too difficult to go in some directions. It takes a supportive group for participants to be willing to take on leadership.

My PDS experience has been much like learning to ride a bike. In the beginning of both, I was very uneasy. When learning to ride a bike, I didn't quite have the feel for how to stay upright. I was afraid of falling, yet I wanted very much to be able to ride. The bike and I were separate machines wanting to work together but not knowing how. I didn't know how the bike worked, so I depended on my dad to hold me up. My dad ran along beside me, trying to let go so I could ride on my own. I kept asking what to do so I wouldn't fall. My dad did not tell me "how" to ride. Instead, he supported me while I got some experience and learned how to pedal, steer, and balance. Eventually I was able to stay up on my own, as long as the road was smooth. Even the smallest rock sent me tumbling to the ground, but I was proud of myself.

Learning to work collaboratively in the PDS was a bit like learning to ride a bike. Marilyn, like my dad, was the supporter. In the beginning, she ran alongside us. Sometimes she would try to let go and let us find our own way, while at other times she held on tightly and gently guided us.

I'm sure there were times when she was just running, not knowing if she should hold tighter or let go. She gave us articles on collaboration to read. I talked to her and to other PDSers. My school was working on a project so I could practice new ways of working together. Eventually I began to have a better understanding of collaboration. I was learning to think about issues in a different way. I was changing my classroom practice to be more collaborative, like the PDS. As long as the collaborative road was smooth and wide, I thought this partnership was great. The problem was that there were simply too many "rocks." We were always falling off the bike. With more experience, more talking, more thinking about collaboration, we get better at maneuvering our way around the rocks.

CHAPTER 7

Theorizing Collaboration: Some Theoretical and Methodological Issues

Marilyn Johnston

This chapter discusses some of the theoretical and methodological issues that have influenced me in my multiple roles as participant, researcher, writer, and editor in this project. It includes discussions of some typical issues of research (for example, the role of the researcher, and issues of representation, subjectivity, and collaborative writing), as well as the theoretical positions that have influenced conceptual aspects of the research and writing of this book.

I initially tried to write separate methodology and theoretical sections for this book. In both, my intent was to situate myself as a participant in this project and as an editor/writer for this book. No matter how many organizing schemas I tried, I was unhappy with them. There were overlaps and tensions that were difficult to sort out when kept in separate sections. I was also uncomfortable separating the methodological questions from their theoretical underpinnings as I tried to position myself in this project. Defining where the methodological aspects of the project are situated as opposed to the epistemological and philosophical claims was problematic for me because it felt arbitrary to pull them apart.

I have taken a different approach to discussing these issues. I address methodological topics (truth claims, representation, the role of the researcher), but also a set of theoretical claims and performative aspects, all with their rough edges and conflicts. My strategy deliberately disrupts the typical form of methodological discussions as it tries to represent my fractured positionings, the uneven influences I have had on the group, and the various effects this project has had on me. I have not tried to tidy up the rough edges or present a polished theoretical position. Rather, this is an attempt to theorize my/our practices, which are still evolving and are purposefully cast in the tensions that are necessarily a part of school/university collaboration.

This discussion takes a circuitous route that raises as many questions as possible while I articulate a point of view as clearly as I can. This approach is necessary because the issues are complicated and my thinking about them disperses in many directions. While a number of the topics in this section have been a part of our group conversations (for example, ethical issues in doing research on ourselves, ways to analyze our data, and the influence of beliefs, gender, culture, and institutional norms on interpretation), they have not been topics others have chosen to write about. The perspectives here are my own, rather than representative of the diversity within the collaborative group.

I use the opportunity of these discussions to explore a post-modern strategy more fully than other places. My intention is to be provocative, deconstructive, and questioning. The book has a flavor of post-structural ideas, but only in spots, and it only partially takes advantage of these ideas. We rarely have time in our collaborative work to spend the time it takes to consider these more esoteric ideas. While I personally see many connections and find these theories useful, the ideas are sometimes in conflict with other perspectives that are more accessible and have more support from my colleagues. Also, I anticipate that some of these ideas may create resistances in some readers which then get in the way of communicating the larger, shared purposes of my colleagues and me. Furthermore, I am also heavily influenced by pragmatism, and there are some uneasy tensions between these two positions.

With these cautions in mind and in a post-modern spirit, I have tried to keep myself uneasy and off balance in this writing and throughout this project in order to push at the boundaries of my own thinking and to explore the possibilities of several kinds of work—political (Nicholson, 1990), imaginative (Greene, 1995), and feminist (Haraway, 1988; Weedon, 1987)—within a collaborative setting. At the same time, I have tried to be sensitive to the needs of colleagues who struggle daily with the demands of teaching, many of whom, in addition, work to educate children engulfed by poverty, violence, and social powerlessness.

IS THIS RESEARCH?

I have from the beginning considered my work in this collaborative project to be my research. While I wanted it to be collaborative, I would have done the research and writing anyway. I have tape-recorded most meetings and conversations, written grant applications to obtain doctoral student assistance for interviewing and data analysis, and written articles (with others and on my own). Many of the audiotapes have been transcribed and shared around. Individuals and small groups working on projects, theses, or presentations have had open access to them. On several occasions, I have, alone or in groups that included me, done more systematic data analysis of some of the transcripts. In addition, I have kept my own field notes and journals.

So far, this looks much like a typical qualitative research project. There were some beginning questions, and new ones emerged in the process. Slowly it has become more and more collaborative. We started with a small group to do a specific research project, but research has become a shared attitude and process that includes everyone. (See the section "The Research Group" in chapter 2 for further discussion on how research has spread from a small group to the whole group.)

A sabbatical gave me additional time to reflect and gave my own ideas time to develop outside the context of group discussion. Frequent E-mail conversations, reading each other's texts, and a trip back home in the middle of the year kept a degree of social interaction alive, even though I was (usually) geographically separated from my colleagues.

SITUATING THE RESEARCHER

Patti Lather said in my reading group one day, "I want to know how you are positioned in relation to your truth claims, not your autobiography." Her statement haunted me as I worked on this section. Laurel Richardson (1995) makes a similar distinction related to qualitative research in general:

> Qualitative writers are off the hook, so to speak. They don't have to try to play God, writing as disembodied omniscient narrators claiming universal, atemporal general knowledge; they can eschew the questionable metanarrative of scientific objectivity and still have plenty to say as situated speakers, subjectivities engaged in knowing/telling about the world as they perceive it. (p. 518)

My goal is to situate my truth claims in order to avoid impressions of objectivity, but I am also cautious not to slide into irrelevant autobiography, what Van Maanen (1988) calls "vanity ethnography." I have used other readers to help me make some of these judgments. I also rely more heavily on other sources here than in other chapters; this strategy helps to ward against the tendencies toward autobiography and situates me in the literatures that have been influential.

Many writers argue for an explicit discussion of the researcher's values. Schratz and Walk (1995) make a typical argument:

> Once we admit that as researchers we hold values that effect the research we do, we have to find ways to scrutinize our actions and our motives more closely. Who the researcher is can no longer be left out of the account without jeopardizing the validity of the enquiry. (p. 5)

Similarly, Visweswaran, in her book *Fictions of Feminist Ethnography* (1994), explains how she is embedded "in a field of power . . . and particular knowledges" (p. 48). She argues for this approach using Donna Haraway's term "accountable positions" (1988). This accountability is "an endeavor to be answerable for what I have learned to see, and for what I have learned to do" (Visweswaran, p. 48). From this point of view, it matters what the researcher has learned (Haraway's "knowledges") and what relationships she or he has to people in her or his research (power). In the same spirit, I try to position myself in a set of knowledges that I have learned and that constitute my particular theoretical/political interests and praxis and to be explicit about power relationships within our collaborative work.

Some feminist theorists have taken this argument a step further and claim that not only should we reveal our personal positionings, but only personal reality is worthy of study, beginning with our own. From this perspective, tendencies toward larger scale theories are rigorously resisted (Stanley & Wise, 1983). I certainly make no claims for larger theoretical positions here; neither is this book intended to create generalizable claims about collaborative work. I/we do, however, move beyond personal experience and try to make sense of our experience as it relates to persistent and perplexing issues that I/we encountered in this collaborative project. As I do this, I try to keep these claims always in question and to resist consistent categories of success/failure and better/worse defined in terms of my experience or that of my colleagues. I hope our experiences are provocative, not prescriptive, pointing to a set of tensions and disruptions rather than stable dichotomies or settled conclusions.

A variety of authors suggest strategies in the spirit of this kind of disruption and maintenance of disequilibrium. Visweswaran (1994) suggests attention to the failure not of our methods, but of our epistemologies. She sees herself as a "trickster ethnographer" who is aware of the impossibilities and limitations of her ability to know even as she uses representation strategies that are inherently flawed (p. 15). There is also Derrida's infamous advocacy for "play" (1989). In this spirit, Patti Lather (Lather & Smithies, 1995), in her study of women living with HIV/AIDS, thinks in terms of "feminist imaginaries of a double science," which "is a notion of inquiry that is both/and and neither/nor science and not-science" (Lather, 1996, p. 5).

SOME TENSIONS

Many tensions have arisen in this project—for example, the differences between group and individual understandings, and between my academic interests and those of my school-based colleagues—and differences considered as sources of conflict or as a way to promote learning. Both the theoretical and performative aspects of these tensions have intrigued a number of us, and we have tried to rethink how we consider these tensions, while remaining critical of using this theoretical construct to describe our experience.

One tension that swims for me just below the surface of this project is how to write about the understandings emerging in group settings and my own theoretical positionings. This tension implicates ways of speaking and/or writing about the group as well as issues of power, about whose ideas influence the group and in what ways. I do not claim to represent my colleagues' ideas or group constructions in "accurate" ways. As a participant in the group, I can "speak with" them as one author, but as I construct this book I am cast in a researcher's role that makes such "speaking with" improbable. I try to be aware of this double role throughout, knowing that my representations are problematic. But this is insufficient. I also want to keep this process of self-reflection under scrutiny, so that these self-investigations are not used to justify my representations, which are then left standing (Lather, 1989). To do this, I try to keep alive the instability of what I/we think we have learned and the limits of representation, which ensures that there is much that cannot be known and/or cannot be spoken (McRobbier, 1982). I want to acknowledge the limits and problems with my own self-interrogations even as I engage in them.

A similar caution exists related to making interpretations. I try throughout to be as explicit as possible about the assumptions that lay behind the interpretations we offer, yet there are layers of assumptions that support interpretation, and I cannot be aware of all of them. As Connolly (1991) argues, "No interpretation can proceed without at least covertly invoking some fundamental presumptions currently underdetermined by reasons and evidence" (pp. 14–15). In practice I proceed as if I am aware of my presuppositions, even as I acknowledge the impossibility of knowing them. Here again is a tension—the tension between the performative aspect of making interpretations and the acknowledgment that we can be only partly aware of the assumptions that guide them. The book rings with more certainty than I believe is justifiable, and yet I hold to a degree of certainty in order to continue the practical work.

Throughout the book we have used the idea of tensions in order to avoid fixed positions or stable dichotomies. The strategy of using tensions in this way provides a more fluid and flexible approach than holding to a single interpretation. However, while the idea of tensions may enhance the fluidity of our thinking, I acknowledge that taking this approach may have obstructed questioning the tensions themselves or obscured other ways of thinking about these issues. How do we both use these categories, question them, and reach for their possibilities while knowing their certain epistemological limits? Judith Butler (1993) suggests "subversive repetition" as a way to keep a non-innocent practice of knowledge production. By this she means using repetition as a strategy in order to reveal and examine one's influence over knowledge production. Repetition is used in order to displace, and this, in turn, allows for further repetition. We do our work even as we know its limitations and impossibilities.

My use of post-modern theories, and particularly arguments within post-structural feminisms, points to another tension—that of my theorizing interests and the different interests of my PDS colleagues. Several graduate students have studied in these areas, but neither my school nor many of my university colleagues are much drawn to these topics. These are not easy areas in which to read; I use a women's faculty reading group to support my reading. Further, I use these points of view to shape a book that is meant to be a collaborative effort. There are a few reasons why this might be considered an imposition. First, schools do not allow for teachers to go to a reading group regularly during school hours. The norms of my institutional context support opportunities and interpretations unavailable to my colleagues. The power typically ascribed to university theories over teachers' concerns then raises questions about imposition, if my framing has undue influence over the shape of "our" book. Nevertheless, these ideas got integrated into our conversations through my participation. They were evident in the issues I raised and in the questions I inserted into our work and relationships. I have kept myself troubled about the influence of my ideas and the interests of my teacher colleagues. I try to remain fearful that my interests will overshadow the teachers' ideas, ideas that were maybe less well articulated because they did not have explicit theories on which to depend.

While I worry about this from a post-structural vantage point, I also know that these are impossible questions. I cannot be self-aware enough to alleviate all imposition. To think that self-awareness and critique can solve the inherent unequal power relations between schools and universities is, of course, naive. Neither can I be lulled into complacency when teachers resist, assert, and lead in their own directions. Rather, I persist with self-reflection even as I know its limits and claim nothing further than limited accounts and partial knowing as my colleagues and I both together and separately reach for necessarily unstable understandings.

Our research presentations provide an instance where my post-modern stance is evident and where I can argue both imposition and collaboration, as well as fathoms of unknowabilities. I have argued persistently for collaborative conference presentations—in particular, the use of formats and texts that honor multiple perspectives and differences within the project. I saw experimental formats as a way to represent the *practices* of collaboration in the *form* of the presentations and to disrupt the conventions of presentations that typically exclude other voices (especially teachers' voices). Teachers initially were not interested in conference presentations, let alone using experimental formats. The obvious tension here for me was between ideas I found personally provocative, and *imposing* these frames on my colleagues, not to mention luring them into university practices of "presenting research" to other academics (there were seldom teachers in the audience).

There are some grounds to argue that my suggestions were used rather than imposed. The presentations themselves rarely turned out as I had anticipated. Other people had ideas to contribute, and there were useful challenges to my own thinking and changes in my understandings that came about through these discussions. The productive and reciprocal aspect of our collaboration that gets highlighted in our presentations can be described (see the chapter 2 section "Academic Aside: Deconstruction and Collaboration") and I can describe changes in my own thinking that were supported at least partially in these activities (see chapter 1, the chapter 2 Academic Aside "Viewing Our History," and chapter 4).

It is less easy to determine how to represent, and even how to understand, the possible negative impact of our conference presentations. I have no doubt, although it is hard to give "evidence," that they excluded and silenced some teachers and administrators. Some PDS members did not ever feel comfortable enough to join a presentation group (out of shyness, intimidation, or lack of time); some ideas did not get nurtured because my experimentally focused perspective prevailed. I also have no doubt that some have felt excluded as presentation groups came back to the larger group with stories of success and evidence of the increased camaraderie which evolved from trips and time spent together. These implications and possible exclusions are the silences behind the successes, the opportunities missed for those who did not participate, and the possible impositions which were unintended, but that I cannot uncover.

In addition to the tension between my perspective and that of others and the tensions between offering/using and imposing my perspective, there were obviously other tensions here. Some were more prominent at one time than at another, and these shift and slide within particular contexts. The same problem occurs at many places in the book. We focus on one set of tensions and consequently hide others. Tensions between tensions are sometimes as perplexing as the dynamics within a particular set of tensions. By highlighting one particular tension, we obscure what might be to others more relevant in the situation. This point is not an argument against the usefulness of tensions but rather an acknowledgment of what has been left unsaid.

FEMINIST RESEARCH METHODOLOGIES

In suggesting the possibilities for a feminist epistemology as a basis for new forms of ethnography, Visweswaran (1994) writes:

> I want to claim shifting identities, temporality, and silence as tools of a feminist ethnography. . . . A feminist ethnographer can consider how identities are multiple, contradictory, partial, and strategic. The underlying assumption is, of course, that the subject herself represents a constellation of conflicting social, linguistic, and political forces. (p. 50)

Feminist epistemological positions, as represented in Visweswaran's claims, helped me to consider my theoretical history and practices. I never seriously considered the multiple positionings I saw in myself as problematic, but I had for some time worried about my lack of consistency. Long after the graduate school pressures to conform to particular points of view subsided, I continued to find myself having conflicting viewpoints in different contexts. This is not to say that I do not have some consistent commitments to some things, particularly some political and educational perspectives. Nevertheless, I often feel chameleonlike in other ways. I find new ideas exhilarating and like to play with these ideas even when they are in conflict with other beliefs of mine. I often find myself wanting to argue on both sides of the issues because I find appealing arguments in several places or fear simple answers which often get used in politically sensitive contexts. Like many women, I have played multiple roles that were often in conflict (wife, mother, teacher, other selves) and I liked moving among these positions even with/because of the conflicts/contrasts they created. I relish a certain amount of ambiguity and see myself as a risk-taker in some areas. This is not a description of a coherent self in a modernist sense.

For a good part of my life, I tried to ignore (or felt guilty about) these variations and conflicts as I hopped from one place to another or straddled more than one position at a time. Feminist epistemologies gave me a theoretical frame for looking at these conflicts and variations in other ways.

These theoretical frames also created spaces for appreciating other points of view rather than trying to resolve or fix differences, especially the differences so vividly evident in collaborative work. I initially tried to fix the well-documented differences between school-based and university-based participants; now I see them as ways to create ambiguity and points of view that push at our ideas and practices. It is a way to give myself and others permission to explore and taste new ideas rather than aiming to create a coordinated set of beliefs or a coherent identity. I have become quite wary of someone who has it all figured out and who does not question his or her own positionings. I distrust the self-assurance of polished arguments that do not also admit to their fallibility and historicity. I no longer want to be convinced of a best way or a right argument; rather, I want to be helped to understand what is behind the argument as well as what is up front, and what is silenced as well as what is spoken. I want authors and dialogue partners to help me in this task; I do not want to be left to my own resources nor left to guess at their intentions.

IN SEARCH OF THE SILENCES

> Silence can be a plan
> Rigorously executed
> The blueprint to a life
>
> It is a present
> It has a history   a form
>
> Do not confuse it
> With any kind of absence.
>   Adrienne Rich (1993, p. 17)

Silence as agency is an idea getting some attention within post-structural feminisms (Minh-ha, 1989; Visweswaran, 1994). With this idea in mind, Visweswaran describes the aim of her research with women as an attempt "to theorize a kind of agency in which resistance can be framed by silence, a refusal to speak. In this my task is partly, as one critic (Spivak, 1988) has suggested, one of 'measuring silences'" (1994, p. 51). Using Bourdieu's notion of heterodoxic discourse (1977), which includes "what goes without saying" and "what cannot be said," Visweswaran argues that we must add an additional category—"what is willfully not spoken."

The idea of "silence as agency" suggests a question that I did not originally consider. I was aware of silences, of teachers who did not speak, did not assert their ideas. I interpreted these silences as shyness, lack of trust, the norms of school cultures to stifle disagreements, or unassertiveness related to gender socialization. These may be other viable interpretations as well, but I have become intrigued with the possibility that teachers willfully choose not to say things, willfully choose not to reveal. Chosen silence in these cases may feel empowering to them because they are withholding their ideas and support and thus hold some sway over outcomes they do not support. My interest is both the possible empowerment from chosen silences and the institutional constraints and structures that create/support them. Of course, resentment and disenfranchisement are possible explanations of silence as well.

In a similar vein, Foucault (1978) argues that there are many kinds of silences:

> There is no binary division to be made between what one says and what one does not say; we must try to determine the different ways of not saying such things . . . . There is not one but many silences, and they are an integral part of the strategies that underlie and permeate discourses. (p. 27)

I have tried to be sensitive to the idea that many kinds of silences undergird our collaborative work, but then understanding why they are there is possible only in the abstract. It is possible that such investigations will do as much to disguise as enlighten.

Seen from an historical context, the silence of teachers, a large percentage of whom are women, is supported by a common socialization process in society. Women are socialized to be silent in authoritarian situations where they feel powerless. At the extreme, battered women rarely speak in resistance to, or speak poorly of, their battering partners; in less extreme cases, passive-aggressive patterns—silences that mask aggression—are stereotypically ascribed to women. Similarly in schools, many norms support teacher silence. "Just close your door and do it anyway," a seasoned teacher told me my first year of teaching, when I wanted to try something of which the principal had vaguely disapproved. I had decided not to attempt it—until this matronly teacher gave me permission. I was being mentored to work, as Adrienne Rich suggests, under the guise of silence.

How does one capture, or pay attention to, the silences in a collaborative project? One of the outcomes of the PDS for many teachers has been to move out of patterns of silence. Working one's way through the silences, however, is disruptive and difficult. In the disruption of these silences there is much to be learned from a research point of view. Often, however, what is revealed cannot be publicly told, and probably more often, what is behind the silences does not get revealed at all.

Sometimes what is behind the silences cannot be revealed because it is invisible to one. Michelle Fine describes her essays in *Disruptive Voices: The Possibilities of Feminist Research* (1992) as attempts to "wedge between women's layers, to hear what has been hidden, swallowed, suffocated, and treasured by, for, and despite women" (p. xii). Wedging between the layers, particularly when it invades the assumptions that define a person's values and sense of worth, raises ethical questions of an enormous range. For example, in our case we built trusting relationships in order to meet a practical goal—

better teacher education. This could be seen as a mask for encouraging personal interrogations and reflections which, unbeknown to participants initially, can cause pain and conflict. We explained the goals of reform, professional development, and inquiry as part of PDS work, but there were no warnings on the label. Caution: asking questions about one's basic beliefs may disrupt the rest of your life. Warning: questions about teaching beliefs may also be connected to beliefs about life more generally; reflect on these questions at the risk of disrupting dearly held beliefs and lifestyles.

For some teachers, asking hard questions about classroom practices and the nature of schooling has meant also asking difficult questions about their partners and lifestyles. If a teacher's role as authoritarian leader of instruction moves toward a more democratic and nurturing relationship with children, he or she may also begin to want the same kind of associations in other relationships; it may be that an authoritarian relationship with a spouse no longer seems as self-evident as it once did. For other teachers, the hard questions slide off their backs like water over a dam.

What is the responsibility of a researcher who knows full well that research questions can provoke these kinds of reflections and openings and the consequent pains of growth and change? One teacher asked me in the midst of some distress over dealing with all the changes that were mushrooming in her teaching practice, "Did you know this was going to happen?" What responsibility is there to remain in a nurturing and supportive role if you wedge into the silences of teachers' professional and personal lives? Is there institutional support for the time and energy it takes to nurture these kinds of relationships, for the time to care and support, for acknowledging and responding to the confluence of people's personal and professional lives? If the institutional support for time is not there, is a researcher nevertheless morally obliged to take the time, probably from his or her own personal life, to be available to the needs of people changing their lives? Wedging into the silences, like opening Pandora's box, means it is difficult to know ahead of time what needs and moral claims will be made of you, the researcher. Further, the moral claims are reciprocal.

If I wedge into other people's silences, the researcher should also be willing to go through this herself or himself. In my case, I decided that I needed also to become vulnerable in the process, not to expect everyone else to go through self-examination and change if I was not willing to do the same. This, in turn, puts similar moral claims on my collaborative colleagues to be there for me, to be a support and helpful critic in the midst of my changes and self-examination. Of course, researchers are protected in some ways because many individuals are not ready for or attracted to this kind of self-reflexivity.

I have wondered at times whether the moral claims inherent in collaborative work are why many of my university colleagues are not interested, or are critical of, such endeavors. To pay attention to these claims takes time and attention not required in other institutional duties. The moral requirements and relationships required for collaboration may also explain why such endeavors are difficult to sustain in university settings, where competition and individual entrepreneurship make it difficult for people to support each other's work.

CONCLUSION

This section is meant to end a bit abruptly and with uneasiness. There are many issues here—mostly unresolved, yet continually intriguing to me. Rather than give answers, I remain fascinated with tensions and fluid categories, which may make this chapter seem unresolved to those searching for conclusions.

I have focused on the post-structural ideas here because they are less explicit than in other discussions in the book. They provide but one of the lenses that I find provocative as I live in this collaborative project. While this project is only a part of my professional life, it has disrupted enough of my thinking that it slides into other places and stimulates new questions about other taken-for-granted aspects of my university work.

Case Studies

We begin part II with case studies of collaboration done in two of our PDS schools. These are the work of teachers who were members of the initial research group, which started at the beginning of the project to study collaboration as it evolved in the individual schools and the project at large. (See the chapter 2 section "The Research Group" for a fuller description.) Some school research teams did not write their histories because of the sensitive and political nature of the struggles they experienced. In other groups, no one had the time or interest to do the writing.

The two cases presented here were developed by teachers in Worthington Estates School (WES) and Second Avenue Elementary School. The first is a suburban elementary school in a middle-class to upper-middle-class socioeconomic neighborhood, a fifteen-minute drive from the university and downtown area. Second Avenue is a densely urban school with more than 95% of its students on free and reduced school lunches, located midway between the university and downtown Columbus. WES is a large school (700 students) with a mostly homogeneous European-American school population and teaching staff. Second Avenue is a small school (300 students) in the oldest school building in the Columbus city schools. The student population is 80% African American and 20% Appalachian students, and the school teaching staff is about 25% African American. WES has computer labs, a music room, many special programs, and lovely playground equipment provided by the PTA. Second Avenue has run-down equipment and facilities, few special programs, little play equipment, and no PTA. Each school has had three principals in five years. Even with the change in principals, WES has had continuity in its instructional program, while Second Avenue has started and stopped many programs mandated by principals and the school district.

It would be hard to find two schools with sharper contrasts. Part of the interest in these case studies is the difference in how collaboration unfolds and the influence of the PDS on these two schools. Teachers at WES generally feel successful. They are proud of their work, parents are supportive and demanding, and teachers are competitive and work hard to develop attractive programs in their classrooms. Test scores of their students are high and reflect the advantages of family support and affluence. Teachers at Second Avenue feel no such support or success. Many parents in their school community are challenged by poverty, violence, and low employment. Before the PDS, the teachers felt isolated from each other and persisted more to survive than to compete with each other. The test scores at Second Avenue are low compared with those of other schools in the district and reflect the lack of advantages of the students.

There are also some interesting similarities between the schools. Both have teachers who have worked with the PDS from the beginning, have taken on significant roles within the PDS, and have made significant changes in their classrooms. Both schools have had teachers who have participated regularly, yet the PDS has had seemingly little influence on their professional lives. Both schools had four or more teachers who spent many hours together working on their case study. Both groups have been challenged by difficult decisions about what and how to tell their stories; both have excluded stories about individuals or issues that were sensitive. In both cases, work on their case studies supported productive inquiry for the teachers as well as adding to our collective understanding of school/university collaboration.

The tone of the two cases is very different. The case written by WES teachers is critical, conflictive, and full of overt analysis of the issues. The case by Second Avenue teachers is tempered and cautious, and the issues are more subtly described. In both cases, I encouraged them to include things they initially wrote but later removed. In only some cases they agreed. The differences between the two cases may be related to the different personalities in the groups, but they are also related to differences between the two schools. The teachers at WES have a bright, cheery environment; the students come to school in good spirits and in general are not challenging of teachers' authority; the parents are supportive although vigilant and sometimes critical; and teachers are presumed competent because students do well on objective tests used to measure school success. The reverse is true in all cases for the teachers at Second Avenue. Their school is in a beautiful old building but is not well kept, and it is in a neighborhood where one worries about safety. All the school doors are locked except a main entrance, and visitors are carefully watched from the office as they come in. Many students come to school challenged by environments where pain and suffering are commonplace. Of course, there are many with strong, loving families. Nevertheless, a significant number of students at Second Avenue bring problems to school that make appropriate behavior and learning difficult for them. These challenges have the tendency to push teachers into control patterns rather than the more elaborate curricular programs of WES. Because test scores are low, teachers feel a sense of failure even when they work hard and students make considerable progress. Their work is seldom acknowledged by parents or other professionals. Second Avenue teachers, in particular, have felt a lack of support from the school district. Before the PDS they had had a string of principals who were unable to deal with the challenges of the school; in the second year the PDS teachers banded together to get the principal "reassigned" with some support from the university. The assertiveness of the teachers and connection with the university has seemingly had an influence on better qualified principal assignments subsequently.

With these differences in mind, the contrasting tone and approaches in the cases are understandable. It is easier to be critical of self and others in an environment where your work is valued and presumed strong. In an environment like Second Avenue, teachers are cautious of criticism, of each other, and of their environment. The school is already stereotyped as problematic, and thus teachers' competence is implicitly questioned. The teachers' needs are for collegiality and support, and they have worked to develop a positive feeling and atmosphere in the school. As a result of their work, the school looks and feels like a different place than it did six years ago. Teachers share ideas, support each other, and solve problems together.

At Second Avenue, it is hard to separate PDS efforts and schoolwide initiatives; they now blend and support each other, and participation in the PDS continues to increase. At WES, the PDS teachers support each other, but there has been little influence on the school as a whole, and participation in PDS is slowly dwindling.

No generalizations about urban and suburban schools can be made from these cases. There are too many variables. It is clear, however, that the urban and suburban characteristics of these schools have had some influence on the teachers, on the differential unfolding of collaboration, on the varied influence of the PDS on school programs, and in the ways these teachers chose to tell their stories.

CHAPTER 8

The Beginnings of Collaboration at Second Avenue Elementary

Reba Bricher, Mary Christenson, Marilyn Hawk, and Jean Tingley, with Brenda Ambrose, Amy Campbell, Lisa Cline, and Bill Lohr

This case study was written by the first four authors and then elaborated and extended into the present by other teachers at Second Avenue. The case captures the dramatic changes that have occurred in this school since they began to work collaboratively. The teachers' collaboration has helped them redress the initial lack of collegiality in the school and thus face together the challenges of working with children who live in poverty. As with any self-study, there are some aspects that are not included because they are politically or personally too sensitive. Nevertheless, their story is richly told with both the setbacks and successes they experienced.

Our story is one of small changes that lead to rather dramatic results. We had no idea of what was to come as we began our collaboration with Ohio State University in the fall of 1990. It started when Marilyn J. called a couple members of our staff to see if there would be any interest in their joining a Quincentenary project. Marilyn J. knew Reba and Jean from a graduate course they had taken with her at the university. We were interested in the possibility of collaboration because we had been isolated in our classrooms for far too long with little help from the outside for the many problems we face each day. Seven of our teachers and our principal agreed to join.

GETTING STARTED

The first meeting of the Quincentenary project was held in our school library in the winter of 1991, and the room was packed with more than 40 people. The chairperson of the city's Quincentenary Committee described the various citywide projects being planned for the 1992 celebrations. "Celebrations" was the term used by the city of Columbus to describe the events occurring around the time of the Quincentenary. In contrast, others used "cultural encounters" in order to be sensitive to indigenous peoples, African Americans, and others who do not see Christopher Columbus's arrival in the Americas as cause for celebration. After a short discussion of this distinction, we discussed the structure of the collaborative group and future plans for the remainder of our first meeting.

Journal Responses

One of our class requirements was to write a weekly journal. For the first and second quarter of our project, everyone was receiving credit. In subsequent quarters, credit was an option for those who wanted it. For credit, there was a requirement to write a weekly journal. The two of us (Jean and Reba) in the research group looked at the journals each week to figure out how our group was feeling about the project. As we looked at the journals over time, and then in retrospect, we could see many changes in our feelings about the project and about collaboration.

This Is Confusing. Teachers' journals from the first evening reflected confusion and frustration over goals and expectations. There was a concern that the project would not benefit our students but was designed to advertise the city of Columbus or perhaps we were just subjects for a university research project. Two comments from the journals:

> We seem to be subjects for study *by* the university, rather than collaborators *with* people from the university. Is this something like an experiment where you put some chimps in a room and they must figure out how to get a banana hanging from the ceiling using a stick and a chair? Will they work together? Will they get the banana? Will they share the banana when they get it? The fact is, we don't even have a banana. There are no clear goals, and in my opinion, an effort without objectives is a waste of effort.

We felt that, given our working conditions and urban student population, our school was at the low end of the academic and political totem poles compared to other schools in the Quincentenary project. However, underlying our concerns was the common feeling that this collaborative effort might support better staff relations within our building. As one teacher expressed it:

> In collaboration we are sharing everything from beginning to end. No one is the leader. We are all on the same level, working toward the

same goal. I'm sure this isn't easy, as many personalities and teaching styles will be intertwined. However, I think it will be rewarding and educational, both personally and professionally.

Finding Some Common Ground. **During** our second class session, we brainstormed ideas for our school project. The journals from this week reflected a sense of accomplishment that we had identified common school problems. We wanted to look at new ways to build self-esteem, create school pride, involve parents in the school, and raise test scores. We decided to do some background reading to learn how other schools that were successfully working with at-risk students had tackled these problems. However, not all members liked this focus. Some wanted a more visible project.

During Thursday class times, we usually met in groups across schools to discuss collaboration using readings that were passed out the week before. We attempted to define collaboration based on our limited knowledge and experience.

As classroom teachers, we tend to do things our own way, partly because we don't have time to exchange ideas with our colleagues. I'm looking forward to working together with our staff group on plans to improve and enrich our classrooms. I believe our collaborative efforts will improve both our teaching and our staff cohesiveness.

Some teachers questioned our ability to work as a group due to the wide range of personalities, teaching styles, and beliefs.

At Second Avenue we have not worked on schoolwide projects . . . . It would be easier for someone to *tell* us what to do, but I think the benefits to be gained by working together warrant the expense of time.

I'm apprehensive about our groups' collaborative abilities. We have a wide range of teaching styles and deep-seated beliefs. I'm wondering how we can all come together on this subject.

Not Enough Time. **For** the next few Thursday meetings we had speakers coming in to talk to us about issues related to the Quincentenary, and we were trying to define our school focus. Journal entries reflected the pressure we were feeling because there was so little time to meet in our school groups during our weekly meetings. There were many questions. Did we need to have more conversations about relationships with other schools in the project? Was a common understanding of the process of collaboration necessary? Did we have shared meanings for the words we were using?

Most of the journals were indicating a sense of progress, but discontentment was also growing. Things were moving too slowly. We had not gone beyond the discussion stage, nor had we set any goals. There was a sense of urgency to begin action. Would we be ready to implement our ideas by the next fall (1991)?

I hope our group can get the ball rolling to be able to focus on our project. So far, there is nothing going on except talking.

This session made me even more hesitant than I felt before. We didn't make any decisions and I feel confused. What are we doing?

Marilyn J.'s journal reflections on our first few meetings were shared with us later:

Thinking back over the first several weeks, especially the third week, it is clear that there are some tense feelings between some of the teachers. As in any school, past histories and differences of opinion are carried into new projects. I don't know the history behind some of the feelings, but they make the discussions tense and uncomfortable. I wonder what it will take to work through these feelings in order to develop the trust necessary for productive collaboration.

Comments similar to Marilyn's were also appearing in the teachers' journals.

Due to past experiences, we're all feeling that we have a hard struggle ahead. We continue to worry about commitment, enthusiasm, relationships, and trust, and if we will ever get this project off the ground.

Feelings about our staff's low morale were vented—perhaps this is a good beginning.

During the sixth class session we spent most of the evening discussing the elements of collaboration. We debated the need and importance of getting to know all the participants. Journal entries were lengthy and reflected many different ideas. Collaboration is a new way of working together, and some teachers were concerned about how to participate.

Sometimes I feel badly after group meetings; maybe I talk too much. I remember [asking], "So, do we agree?" when it might not have been my place. I'm too used to treasurer, secretary, vice president, and president, I guess. The readings keep saying that collaborative roles will (should) occur naturally. I don't want to be pushy.

Several teachers were positive about sharing ideas and information with other schools, but they felt that the collaborative framework was too time consuming.

> Most of us worry about the time needed to successfully accomplish our task and question supportive and continued leadership in our school. There also still seems to be some concern that all members will do their part.

> We discussed a few concerns drawn from our last journal entries— time demands, continuity, and administration changes. These are all serious concerns for us and weigh heavily on our minds.

Some comments had glimmers of hopefulness:

> Just working together and creating some positive feelings, exciting ideas, and building-wide activities will make a big difference. We're asking kids to be positive in school while we're not so positive ourselves.

> So let's quit griping about behaviors on Thursday nights and get busy! Let's try some new things.

One teacher was openly hopeful:

> I'm actually beginning to look forward to our meetings because I can see much learning and fun taking place "down the road" for the children—and for us!

Several teachers began to mention the positive outcomes of getting to know each other better. They saw collegiality as something that supported closer relationships and created a sense that everyone was sharing similar problems and concerns about our school and our students.

> In these few short weeks, I personally feel a closer relationship with my school staff than I've felt for four years in the building. Just getting to know them a little better by interacting more has been very beneficial.

> I have sensed that members are learning that we all share the same school concerns and have a common desire to focus upon a course of action that will truly make a change in our daily teaching. In general, we are becoming better acquainted.

Marilyn J.'s journal also reflected this:

> The thing that really knocked my socks off was a comment made by
> Reba. I asked at the end of the session why the group was so different
> this week. Reba said, "We know each other better." As I thought
> about this, I was amazed. This staff has worked together, some of
> them for a considerable time, and yet it has taken this kind of project
> and conversation for them to feel like they know each other.

By the sixth week, concerns over how journals were being used were
surfacing, especially with regard to issues of confidentiality. The research
group were looking at the journals in order to study what was happening
across the schools, but this openness made teachers feel uneasy.

> We are still somewhat concerned about our journals being made
> public. We want to be open in our communication of thoughts and
> ideas; however, we must be discreet. This is a difficult situation.

We've Got It. By the next week, we had decided on the theme *Explora-*
tions, and the journals reflected a sense of hope that our project would include the whole school and generate excitement for students and staff. We
decided the next week to start meeting on Tuesdays in addition to the Thursday class. We also scheduled a presentation for the next staff meeting.

Concerns began to surface that several people were monopolizing the
discussions, which led to a conversation about whether we should have a
facilitator. We decided that such a role would not be collaborative. We also
talked about whether there can be a true collaborative relationship in our
present traditional school structure.

Marilyn J. spent many hours with us in our planning meetings and was
careful not to impose her ideas on us. We often held back waiting for her
suggestions, but then no one in the group seemed to want to assume a leadership role. One teacher wrote about Marilyn's presence:

> I like Marilyn J.'s role in our group. The field notes are helpful, too
> [Marilyn's notes from each meeting were passed out to the group the
> next week]. Some of the comments have been very well put but to
> the point. I can see where an "innocent bystander" in our group will
> be an asset.

Reflections on the First Quarter. Looking back over the quarter, there is a
rise and then a fall in the groups' attitudes and enthusiasm. This felt like
the rise and fall of ocean waves, accompanied by an undercurrent of skep-

ticism, hostility, and concern. In the beginning we were skeptical—other projects had come and gone with little effect. Slowly a sense of hope developed that we could make a difference for our students and their families. These feelings were soon replaced with apprehension and doubt because the collaborative process was so ambiguous. There was still some suspicion about the university participants' roles and the *real* purposes for this class.

Also in question was the ability of our staff members to work together. We were not used to working collaboratively. We had to establish communication channels and build trust. As the quarter progressed we became better acquainted, and we began the slow process of building closer relationships that would facilitate collaboration. At times this was extremely difficult. Most of us had spent our previous professional lives isolated in our classrooms; working collaboratively was threatening, and we had little sense of how to work together differently. There was also a continuing concern that our principal was not attending the meetings and was not very supportive.

CONTINUING OUR COLLABORATION

Our primary reason for joining the collaborative project had been to improve the climate of our school. We wanted our project to involve the whole staff in a way that would encourage but not dictate participation. During the spring of 1991 we presented our ideas to the staff, and their response was favorable. The teachers suggested countries to study for our explorations theme, and we laid out a schedule for the year. The core group (those attending Thursday meetings) offered to provide resources, suggest classroom activities, and coordinate school activities.

Schoolwide Activities

Our first project was a great success. We organized a homework assignment for all the students asking them to generate a list of explorers. The compilation was displayed in the main hallway. It was quite extensive and included both explorers in the traditional sense, such as Christopher Columbus and Neil Armstrong, and explorers of ideas, such as Martin Luther King, Jr., and Albert Einstein. Individual teachers used the list as a starting point to study what explorers do.

There was a growing spirit of collaboration and better communication among teachers, as we'd planned during spring quarter. There was something positive to talk about, rather than just the same old problems. By contrast, our principal was only very passively involved. He occasionally asked, "What do you want me to do?", but instead of taking part in the collaborative group, he chose to stay on the outside. We felt that he positioned himself this way to maintain his power better.

To end the school year on a positive note and to generate enthusiasm for the exploration project the coming year, we organized an assembly featuring a visit by the "World Walker," Steven Newman, who was living in Ohio. One of our core group members had recently read his book *World Walk* (1989). He accepted an invitation for May, and we planned many schoolwide activities to prepare for his visit. We made a large map for each class to show the countries he had walked through on his around-the-world journey. Students drew characters to fill up the maps, similar to the format of the *Where's Waldo* books (Hardford, 1987). A signature stick figure with a walking stick, hat, and backpack, found throughout Mr. Newman's book (1989), was placed somewhere on each of the maps. The maps were displayed in the gym so the students could "search for Steven."

Copies of Newman's book were purchased, and teachers shared his stories with the students, who responded enthusiastically. Their enthusiasm was perhaps the reason the students' behavior was not ideal during the assembly. Mr. Newman had to stop repeatedly to wait for quiet. Our principal should have been at the assembly to help curb the overly exuberant behavior. His absence was another example of his lack of support. In spite of these problems, our kickoff activities in general were very positive experiences for everyone involved.

Project or School Issues?

While things were going very well, we also sensed an underlying tension between those who wanted a visible project for the Quincentenary and those who wanted to concentrate on the problems of our school—for example, working with at-risk students, staff morale, and administrative support. After extensive conversations, we decided to continue our study of countries as well as focus attention on solving school problems. We also wanted to develop ideas for writing some funding proposals. Rather than make a choice that would alienate one group or another, we decided to work on all these things.

As we spent hours together struggling with our shared problems, we were developing a greater sense of trust. We were more open with each other in sharing our many daily problems and frustrations.

At the end of the quarter, we were accepted as a PDS project. As a result, we now had a certification program to plan and MEd interns to supervise beginning in the fall. Our tasks seemed overwhelming.

THE SUMMER—CLASSES, PLANNING, WORRIES

Immediately after school was out (June 1991), most of our core group attended an enjoyable week-long workshop on cultural encounters and the Columbian Quincentenary. We learned a lot about Christopher Columbus, the historical period in which he lived, and the controversies surrounding the historical accounts and public discourse about Columbus.

The following week was intense. We met as the whole group to plan for our PDS activities that were to start in the fall. Originally the schedule was to be group planning for the PDS in the mornings and school planning for the Quincentenary projects in the afternoons. Planning for the PDS, however, took so much time that we had little left for school plans. Constructing a framework for a PDS was difficult. We had no models and had to clarify what we were trying to accomplish.

The planning week was frustrating because we expected to have time to develop plans and work on curriculum for Second Avenue. We decided at the end of the week to do some research during the summer (some of us were getting credit for independent studies). We drew up a list of topics related to areas needing improvement at our school, and each member chose one. In July, we met for a potluck meal at Mary Collins's house and spent four hours talking about our readings and ideas. We talked about cross-age tutoring, multi-aged classrooms, year-round schools, and parent involvement in urban schools. We also spent considerable time wondering whether the principal would be returning, and if so, what level of support we might receive for our project. As with a number of other meetings, we discussed many ideas but did not leave with any action plans. We continued to feel like the poor stepchild of the district because our school lacked the support and resources other PDS schools seemed to have.

In retrospect, we recognized that there was a lack of leadership within the group and everyone was reluctant to initiate action. The overwhelming problems of dealing with at-risk children were so great that we were not able to come to any consensus about where to start. We also felt we lacked the power to make broad-ranging decisions that would be accepted by our colleagues or the principal.

STARTING UP AGAIN: FALL QUARTER

Many things were going on simultaneously during the fall quarter of 1991. We were excited, but also a bit overwhelmed. PDS interns arrived in our building, there were new district required initiatives beginning, and we wanted to initiate some of the ideas we had read about during the summer, especially cross-age tutoring, increasing parent participation, and involving community agencies in the school. It was hard to set priorities or decide what should be done first, so we tried to do them all. A continuing lack of support from the principal complicated our efforts.

Tensions With the Principal and District Initiatives

Our principal had submitted a $5,000 proposal to the State Department the previous spring to support an "effective schools process." This sets out guidelines for increasing school effectiveness. The principal was excited about this particular approach and was a workshop leader in other parts of the country, but as teachers in his building we had little idea of what the process entailed or what we were expected to do. The principal had asked for our input before submitting the proposal, but the grant did not reflect any of our ideas or suggestions. Many of the guidelines overlapped with our PDS goals. Rather than combine them, however, the principal used activities supported by the "effective schools" funding to undermine PDS efforts. For example, we had planned some after-school sessions to invite parents to some make-it-and-take-it workshops that would help them make games and other materials to use with their children at home; a short time later, the principal asked a non- PDS teacher to initiate similar workshops, which led to confusion on the part of the parents and bad feelings among the staff. We eventually got coordinated and worked together on this project, but it took time and energy that could have been spent in more productive ways.

During this period, the school board brought in a new superintendent. He adopted "effective schools" as a process for initiating the improvements he planned for the school district. The principal appointed a committee of teachers who were to attend a workshop before school started. At this district workshop, the committee, including the principal, was to begin work on a mission statement for Second Avenue based on guidelines given to the principals. Our principal left early during a coffee break without giving us the materials we needed to begin this process.

The effective schools committee (ESC), which included four people from the PDS group, was to meet throughout the year. It turned out that there were only two meetings in the fall, and they were primarily lectures by individuals from the State Office of Education telling us how to do our jobs. We felt there was no respect for our experience or abilities; the communication was strictly one way.

In the fall, the principal's grant proposal was approved, and we spent some of each Tuesday planning meeting, which should have been used to discuss PDS topics, trying to decide how to use the money. We had many suggestions, but they were ignored. The principal decided on a training program and substitutes released half the school at a time to attend. All teachers, aides, secretaries, food service workers, and the custodian were required to attend, but the principal never did. There were mixed reactions to the workshops, but in general, we felt the money could have been better spent.

Initiatives to Work With Parents

On Tuesdays we talked a lot about how to increase parental involvement. This was a concern of our PDS group; it was also a major emphasis of the effective schools process; and it is strongly supported in the professional literature as critical to school achievement. We suspected that one reason parents were reluctant to get involved were past negative experiences with the school that had created a them-versus-us atmosphere. To help work against this attitude, we planned an informal get-together after school. We each called some parents and personally invited them to share refreshments and discuss ideas and concerns about the school.

We deliberately did not set a formal agenda for this meeting so that we could be casual and get to know each other on a more personal level. We were stunned when the meeting started and the principal introduced a speaker, a volunteer from another Columbus school, who talked at length about volunteering and then passed out a parent survey. We were embarrassed because we had promised people an informal event and because some of the parents we invited did not have the reading and writing skills needed to fill out the written questionnaire. They had not come expecting to be pressured into service or humiliated. Although the turnout for the meeting was good, the next two meetings were poorly attended. We are certain this was due at least in part to the way the first meeting was handled.

Working With the Interns

Fall activities for the PDS began before school with a potluck dinner so that everyone could meet the interns. We ate and talked, and then each school gave a brief overview of its collaborative projects and school cultures. A number of interns expressed interest in beginning the school year with us and made arrangements to visit our classrooms the first week of school. Some of the interns volunteered to help with setting up classrooms before school opened. Some teachers were reluctant to share the tasks because they had specific ways of doing things and did not want to take the extra time to explain details. Others welcomed the extra help.

At our first Thursday meeting, we met with the interns who had been assigned to our classrooms. We were supposed to have time to get acquainted, but instead, our principal, on one of his rare visits, lectured us for the allotted time and then left abruptly. His spiel contained the usual platitudes and empty promises we had heard too many times to take seriously. We had little time left to get acquainted with our interns. We were angry and frustrated, and the interns were a bit bewildered.

Two interns were assigned to each of our classrooms for two days a week for their fall field experiences. Because each of us had different experiences with our interns, we decided to record our reflections separately.

Marilyn Hawk: As the quarter proceeded, the interns did their methods course activities very nicely; however, it was a bit disruptive with the frequent pulling-out of small groups and individuals. I remember thinking, "It's a good thing I am a flexible person." The children were more excitable on the days the interns were there and did not treat them with respect. Sometimes while I was teaching, the interns would sit and carry on personal conversations instead of helping students, as I'd suggested. Perhaps I expect too much from them as novices.

Reba Bricher: I sometimes felt resentful and put-upon by the extra work involved and disappointed that assignments couldn't be more closely aligned to my curriculum. In many respects, I viewed the placement of these students as only slightly different from the usual placement of student teachers. We had expected collaborative interaction between methods course instructors and cooperative teachers, but this did not materialize.

Mary Christenson: My experience with my two interns was not very satisfactory. First, finding time for them to finish their many university assignments caused a major disruption, because they were either unwilling or unable to integrate their activities into my program. The biggest issue for me was the fact that children's behavior was always much worse on the days my two male interns were there. One [intern], in particular, frequently did things that undermined my classroom management. He would joke and play with children who had been asked to listen to directions or line up quietly to leave the room. After a long intervention process with the GA at Second Avenue, we found him another placement. Once he left, the other student finished the quarter with few problems. Having an intern this first year did not provide the extra help in the classroom that I had expected.

Jean Tingley: As I listened to other teachers talk, I realize how lucky I was to have two very mature, self-directed interns in my classroom. They fit into the routine of the class rather than disrupting it. They worked with individual students whenever they were not doing their assignments. One intern chose one of my very low students and worked with him daily on reading and writing. She found books on his level and did an excellent job of building his self-esteem. My other intern circulated more but was always available for the extra help so often needed by my students. Because of the benefits they provided, I have a very positive opinion of my involvement in the PDS.

Our individual experiences reflect many of the general problems we were having in this first year as a PDS, including too many uncoordinated assignments that the students had to do for their methods courses. As we began our collaboration in teacher education, we had many growing pains and did not yet know how to coordinate university course requirements and school curricula and schedules. It is out of these frustrations that we made changes during the year and for the next year as well.

Thursday Meetings

By the time our PDS activities began in the fall quarter, we no longer called our Thursday meeting a "class." While many teachers were receiving credit, there was much more variety in the kinds of work and types of credit received (workshop and graduate credit). Most graduate studies credit projects were self-defined action research or writing projects related to the case studies. Gradually we started calling our Thursday gatherings "meetings" in order to reflect the more collaborative nature of our work together. The name change was deliberate in order to make a sharper contrast between what we were doing and the hierarchical structure of university courses where professors plan the agenda and set the requirements.

Our Thursday night meetings seemed to be totally taken up with PDS concerns and problems. Simple organizational questions took hours. Learning to work collaboratively was not easy. We were very discontented because we felt this was taking time away from the things in our school that we believed were more important. Progress on individual school Quincentenary projects was reported each week, and it seemed that other schools were making headway while we were floundering. We seldom had time for planning our school project on Thursdays, so our group continued to meet on Tuesdays after school.

Thursday meetings usually began with mixed group discussions based on topics generated by the steering committee. The groups were a combination of teachers, interns, GAs, and principals (except for ours). The topics varied. Should we continue the requirement that teachers with interns attend Thursday night? Can collaboration work without continual conversation and group decision making? We also had many speakers, including the dean from the college and instructors from the methods courses. The last half hour was devoted to issues related to supervision of the interns. From 7:30 to 8:30 the research group met. Reba, Marilyn (Hawk), and Jean were part of this group.

During the quarter there were many problems with coordinating the methods course requirements with classroom curricula and schedules. Out of frustration, at one of the last meetings of the quarter when Marilyn J. was out of town, we drafted a letter to the university instructors requesting their presence at a meeting early the next quarter. It seemed that people felt freer to take charge when Marilyn J. wasn't there. As calmer heads prevailed, the letter was not sent, but the instructors were told about its contents and some changes were made.

There were a number of ways in which our principal continued to be unsupportive of PDS. For example, one of our teachers wanted to co-teach the social studies methods course, but there always seemed to be some problem getting her a substitute. The principal gave many reasons why this happened, including that the substitutes had not been approved "downtown." Teachers from other schools were being released, so we assumed that he had not requested a substitute.

Biting Off More Than We Could Chew

On Tuesdays, we were also working with one of the PDS doctoral students, Denise Dallmer, to write a proposal for a "home-based team" which would consist of a social worker, an educational specialist, and an alcohol and drug abuse counselor. This team would be based at the school and would provide "linkages between the family, community, and the school." Mary, Denise, and Marilyn J. agreed to meet over winter break to write the proposal.

Our time commitments were expanding with our ideas. We were working with the interns and attending two or three PDS meetings per week, plus the effective schools planning meetings. In addition, there were classroom responsibilities, grade level meetings, district meetings, and other duties. Some weeks we had meetings before and after school almost every day. Many of us felt our teaching suffered, and we were exhausted.

Before leaving for winter break we were given a huge packet of information about effective schools, including a form from the school district office outlining the areas to be included in a "roadmap." The roadmap was to be based on the mission statement and developed by the staff to address problems identified from a building survey. We were to take the packet home over the holidays and come back with ideas. The roadmap was due January 31, 1992.

The amount of time we spent planning this quarter was extraordinary, and yet making decisions in the group was still painful because it was so hard to do. We were tentative in meetings for several reasons. The relationships between PDS participants still felt fragile, and we also worried about keeping positive relationships with non-PDS teachers in the building. Working in a school like Second Avenue is hard enough without alienating people one is trying to work with. If you're all in a boat trying to row in the same direction, you don't want to do anything that will result in someone not wanting to row with you. We also continued to feel cautious about interactions with the principal because he was still the boss. On top of everything else, he had begun threatening us that we would lose our jobs if our students' test scores did not go up.

All these things made us tentative. If someone suggested an idea, no one wanted to disagree because it might cause conflict. Some of us were also afraid that if we did stick our neck out, no one would support us. Our lack of assertiveness meant that we had no leadership in the group and so progress was slow.

WINTER QUARTER—GLIMMERS OF HOPE

After a much too brief winter break (1992), we were back at school. Two of our teachers began co-teaching methods courses one day a week. Marilyn J. had worked out the previous substitute problem by setting up arrangements directly with the district administration. Columbus does not provide half-day substitutes, which was what was designated for co-teaching. Coverage for the remaining afternoons was available to us as a staff. We decided to make the substitutes' afternoon time available for other teachers in the building. We were hoping that this would promote a better sense of schoolwide involvement and improve school climate. Teachers used the time to visit other schools, make parent contacts, do library research, attend conferences, and plan for schoolwide activities. This release time was a very positive benefit of the PDS. Mary Christenson writes of her experience co-teaching:

> My participation as a co-teacher rekindled my enthusiasm for children's literature and provided me with a set of new book titles and ideas to use in my classroom. Co-teaching a college course was a new and exciting experience for me, but after this initial attempt I decided not to volunteer again unless certain circumstances changed. My second-grade students became increasingly resentful about my being gone each week. The district was unable to send a consistent substitute each week, and the children were often uncooperative. Essentially, the children wasted one morning a week, and I had to deal with discipline problems each time I returned. Also, the time spent plan-

ning for co-teaching and for the substitute was time taken away from class preparation. I would consider co-teaching again only if I could plan with a consistent substitute.

During one of the planning meetings at school, we met with our school's area supervisor. This was the first time we felt anyone from the central office was willing to listen to our concerns. Marilyn J. had talked with him earlier about some of our concerns and invited him to the meeting. We discussed the procedure we had been following to develop the effective schools roadmap requested by the superintendent. Although our principal was supposed to be an expert on this process, the correct guidelines had not been followed. We also talked about frustrations we had about his leadership in the school. The area supervisor's interest and follow-up were very encouraging. As a result, the principal began attending some of our meetings and scheduled some resource people to meet with us related to topics of interest. However, in general, communication problems continued much as before.

Other projects were developed. Mary Collins arranged for a Grandparents' Day and luncheon. The turnout was tremendous. Reba brought in a speaker on child abuse for a second parents' meeting and luncheon. This went so well that we planned a third luncheon for later in the spring.

We had fewer interns in the building during winter quarter, and feelings were more positive. Expectations were clearer and scheduling and requirements were more flexible. Although time consuming, our planning on Thursday nights was having some positive effects in ironing out some of the problems that had developed.

By the end of the quarter, we recognized some positive aspects of our PDS involvement. The district office showed interest in our concerns, intern assignments had gone more smoothly, and the release time for professional development was relished. Nevertheless, some teachers were disappointed when they learned they did not get an intern for the spring student teaching quarter. After all the time and energy they had invested, they were offended that no one had chosen their classrooms. Our school is the most densely urban school in our PDS, and we sometimes feel like interns are intimidated by our challenges or that we are considered less effective teachers because our students' test scores are very low.

IT'S SPRING QUARTER

During spring quarter of 1992 there were many problems with Thursday meetings because school activities conflicted with attendance. Some felt the meetings offered little in return for the time spent. Agendas were constantly being revised, and this caused confusion about where and when we were to meet. The research group rarely met as a whole because small groups were busy preparing for conference presentations. Supervision problems on the agenda were seldom discussed. The steering committee was forced to make decisions because the whole group was not meeting regularly. Two schools did not have representatives on the steering committee, causing more communication problems. Not all schools had access to E-mail, and we had not developed good ways to share information with everyone. Our in-school planning meetings were reduced in number due to district-wide staff development meetings, vacation breaks, and extra sessions to work on the roadmap.

Over the university's spring break, changes occurred; each core group member got a student teacher, after all. Three of the six interns who had been in the building previously chose to come back for their field experience, which pleased us.

Things went more smoothly during spring quarter with intern placements. Both interns and teachers had a better idea of what to expect. Having the same intern in the classroom every day for the student teaching quarter gave more continuity to the program, and the students began to react more cooperatively with them.

While placements were going better, other demands continued to be overwhelming. We had to set up supervision conferences with our interns and the doctoral student in our building. We were finishing the "effective schools" roadmap. Marilyn J. was pushing us to use the "copious free time" provided by our interns to plan parent meetings. However, we were not supposed to leave interns alone too long, because every class had many students with behavior problems. Throughout all this, Reba, Jean, and Marilyn Hawk were trying to work on the first installment of this epic. We welcomed the end of the school year.

CONCLUSIONS

We began writing this history of Second Avenue during the second summer. Since then, we have repeatedly come back to our case study to do some rewriting and editing and to think more about how things have changed since we began our PDS work. We have distilled our separate memories and understandings into a collective one through hours of discussing, arguing, and rethinking the events that have transpired since we began five years ago.

Building Community Takes Time

We view our involvement with a mixture of pride in having brought about some changes at Second Avenue and frustration that it has taken so much time.

When we began, there was little sense of community among the teachers in our building. We were working with the fourth principal in five years, which led us to believe that the school system did not care about our school. Our students' test scores were rock bottom, all of us had children with behavior problems in our classrooms, the building was poorly maintained, and our equipment was old and limited. We seized the opportunity to work with the university and other schools. We were hoping the university would provide us with answers on how to improve our school.

Little did we realize how long it would take to make collaboration work. We were accustomed to doing what we were told, rather than coming up with our own plans. Innovation at the building level had not previously been encouraged. We now expect that innovation is part of our professional growth and development.

Freedom from isolation has been one of the most important benefits of our PDS involvement. We now talk to each other freely about our concerns and realize we can make a difference by working together. We feel empowered to initiate change. While the university has not provided us with answers to our problems, they have provided support for change and interns to work in our classrooms. Although not all intern placements have worked well, most were successful. Our students have received more individual attention, and they have been exposed to new ideas (as we have). In order to explain our own theories and practices with the interns, we have had to examine our own teaching. In the beginning, the interns' questions felt threatening. Now we encourage them to think critically and ask questions, and as a result we are learning and growing professionally.

A Changing School Culture

We see the results of our participation daily in the improved building climate and collaborative planning. We have pushed ourselves to investigate ways of improving our building. We have developed new ways of communicating and working together. This case study completed August 1992 is an example. The four of us working together were forced to examine our beliefs so we could articulate and defend them. Our collegiality and reflections have been made meaningful and have had lasting and tangible results. For example, Jean and Reba teach third grade together. We freely disagree as well as share ideas. When we're planning, we assume that we should work together. Before PDS, we always worked by ourselves. Within the teacher group in general, there is support when anyone is going through a difficult time. No matter what kind of problem comes up—in the classroom or in our personal lives—others are there to help out. We have a genuine sense of collegiality in our building that did not exist before PDS.

CURRENT PERSPECTIVES

We conclude this case study during the summer of 1996 with some re-flections from case study authors as well as some of our more recent PDS colleagues. First, some comments from our case study authors.

Marilyn Hawk: It has been quite a while since I last read our case study. As I reread it, I thought, "How depressing, and how did we survive those first years of collaborating?" That is when I began to realize what a difference being a part of the PDS has made. Not only has it made an individual difference; it has also helped to change the culture of the school. We're now like family. We don't close our doors, teach, do the necessary "school stuff," and then go home exhausted, as we did when I first came to Second Avenue. We now talk with and support each other constantly. We have a wonderful administrator who works with us. We do many interesting things with our children and parents. We take workshops and courses together as a staff. We plan work and do some socializing together. And guess what? We still have the same clientele, but we seem happier. Things seem to run more smoothly, and we see significant improvement in reading skills, too.

Mary Christenson: My teaching methods and my attitude about learning have changed tremendously since I first became involved in the PDS. Initially, I was a traditional teacher in spite of training to the contrary at The Ohio State University back in the early 1980s. I had reached a learning plateau. Satisfied that I had learned what I needed to earn an income, I accepted what was common practice in the places where I taught without questioning the value of those practices. My priorities were to satisfy the requirements of my employers and fit in with the other teachers. While I am, of course, still anxious to keep my job, I am much more likely to take risks and make changes.

Learning is now fun for its own sake, not just as a means to an end. I have more confidence in my abilities to be a reflective teacher who can defend my classroom practice based on sound theory and professional experience. I feel that I have become a leader rather than a follower because of my PDS involvement. New teachers in our building do not recognize what a dramatic change has occurred. They take our open sharing of ideas and concerns for granted.

REBA BRICHER: When I came to this school 13 years ago, the staff ex-changed pleasantries, went into their classrooms, closed their doors, and then left school soon after the dismissal bell. What they did behind their closed doors seemed a big secret.

JEAN TINGLEY: On the afternoon that I came to Second Avenue for a job interview, I was struck by the fact that most teachers were leaving the building at 3:45. When I started teaching at Second Avenue, teachers were very friendly and helpful—to a point. There was, however, little or no discussion of what went on in their individual classrooms.

REBA: As I reflect back on my PDS involvement, after taking a break from PDS for about a year and a half, I am reminded of all that our staff has gained from being a part of this group. The PDS has helped to bring about considerable change in our thinking and the way we work.

JEAN: I agree. I credit our involvement in the PDS for much of the improvement in our school. Our PDS involvement encouraged us to respect each other and our differing ideas.

REBA: Because of PDS, we have opened our classroom doors, let down our guard, and become acquainted. We've discovered that supporting each other, planning together, and sharing ideas not only lightens the workload but can be fun.

Teachers recently coming to Second Avenue and reading this case study have been surprised by the dramatic changes that have occurred in our school. We asked them to write their responses to our case study as more recent colleagues at Second Avenue.

Amy Campbell: Reading this case history made me realize that many changes have occurred at Second Avenue in the past five years. I can't imagine working on a school project without principal and staff support. The first PDS group had to face many obstacles.

All of the hard work that has been done at Second Avenue has made a difference. We now have a principal who is actively involved with school projects. For the most part, the staff works well together. PDS has given many of us the opportunity to explore educational issues. We are a better school and I am a better teacher due to the PDS program.

Brenda Ambrose: As a newer staff member, [I find] it interesting to read about the transformations that have occurred at Second Avenue. A sense of frustration is still apparent as we spend countless hours making plans to initiate change. Unfortunately, some staff members still are not willing to invest the extra time or try innovative practices in their classrooms. This hinders the rest of the staff as we try to work together and plan.

One year in the PDS has helped me to view myself as a reflective teacher. I am now more able to take risks, try new things, work as a team, and justify my classroom practices as they relate to theory. At Second Avenue, the staff and principal welcome and offer support to those pursuing professional growth opportunities.

Lisa Cline: As a new teacher at Second Avenue, I knew about the PDS program. Although it sounded interesting, I was a new mom and just getting back into teaching. I was asked to help out by taking a team of interns for early placement. I did not realize how interesting it would be to have interns in my classroom. We formed a bond as a team and decided to stick together the whole year. I have to admit, however, that my heart was not in the Thursday night meetings. They were full of confusion and bickering. The bickering got better, but the confusion lasted. We decided things one week only to have them changed the next week. Things became more interesting when we got into our project groups. My group was studying whole language with an emphasis on spelling. It was great to have a chance to talk to my colleagues about new things we were trying in our classrooms and to get suggestions when things didn't go quite right. As we all know, there isn't enough time during the day to talk about ideas.

Bill Lohr: During the 1995–1996 school year, I taught a fourth-grade class at Second Avenue. This was my first year at Second Avenue and I was quite surprised to learn about some of the difficult challenges the teachers faced during early implementation of the PDS program. The contrasts between those early years of collaboration and the present school climate are amazing.

My impression of Second Avenue is that it is a very positive place to work, where it is safe to share ideas and ask for help. The teachers focus on themes and units within grade-level teams. Teachers are enthusiastic amid the challenges of teaching in an inner-city school. They have helped me to feel comfortable asking for help while still being valued as an important contributor to the school's success.

CHAPTER 9

A Case Study of Collaboration at Worthington Estates Elementary

Tom Adams, Rosario Galarza, Kathy Nalle, and Lisa Westhoven, with Kathy Barkhurst, Kathy Davenport, and Sue Knuebel

This second case study raises many of the same issues as did the case study of Second Avenue, but there are stark differences between the schools. While teachers in both schools were aiming to establish collaborative norms within their school groups, many variables influence the particular way collaboration evolves at Worthington Estates.

This is a true story about how our school, Worthington Estates Elementary (WES), worked with The Ohio State University (OSU) and five other elementary schools on a collaborative project. Writing this story has been a long and arduous process. As can be seen by the long list of authors, this story has many perspectives. To help us better represent everyone's perspective, we wrote this story using a rich database of journals written by the project teachers in our school and audiotapes of meetings and conversations. Two of us (Lisa and Rosario) started the writing for this case, and then two others (Tom and Kathy) joined the writing team, adding to the complexity of telling this story. Marilyn Johnston gave ongoing feedback and wrote in her perspective. Others have since commented on the text. When the case study was completed, it was 40 pages long, but intelligible only to those involved. So we (Lisa and Kathy) started again, and then we had feedback from the other authors.

We hope we have produced something that others will enjoy reading and that they may profit from our experience. While many aspects of our participation were painful and conflictful, we also learned a great deal. Even though we shared these experiences, we did not all come away with the same interpretations. We hope this story reflects our multiple perspectives and understandings.

GETTING STARTED

As with all good stories, the setting, characters, and plot are important. Our story begins in the fall of 1990, when Ohio State University was soliciting schools to join the Quincentenary project. Our principal and two university professors planned a meeting to discuss the possibility of our school joining. The Columbian Quincentennial was a relevant topic because we are located in Columbus, Ohio, the largest city in North America to be named after Christopher Columbus. The entire metropolitan area was in the process of preparing for the Quincentennial, so it was only fitting that children be exposed to a curriculum that reflected multiple perspectives about Christopher Columbus.

As is usual for our school, everyone was invited to attend the meeting. About 15 teachers came for a variety of reasons: obligation, university credit, interest in the Quincentenary project, curiosity, or refreshments. During this meeting, we were given information, yet specific requirements were not spelled out. This was aptly reflected when one teacher wrote later in her journal:

> We knew this was tied into the Quincentennial and involved OSU, and the rest was a mystery. It was so new that I got the impression Marilyn (the university professor) was unorganized and noncommittal.

Little did we realize at the time how the project described at this meeting would cause joys and struggles and lead to changes in many aspects of our professional and personal lives.

Maybe we should say from the beginning that our staff has never been a close-knit family. Our school is physically large and sprawling (700 students and 40 teachers). Communication between faculty members is limited and often superficial. One of the core group (teachers who joined the Quincentenary project) wrote in her journal:

> Our WES group is not only full of different personalities, which in a sense I think is good, but we all have different interests and expectations of not only what we should do but also final products.

In January we joined the Quincentenary project with five other schools and the university to begin our collaborative adventure. For the first meeting, the room was crowded, with clusters of conversations going on in each school group. This made it seem as if other schools knew what was going on while we were in the dark.

The project was also to be a school/university research study, so we were asked to write weekly journals. Two of our teachers (Lisa and Rosario) joined the research group and we turned our journals into them each week. Initially the weekly journals were full of excitement, stimulation, overwhelmed feeling, and a lot of self-doubt. This kind of collaborative work was new and different for all of us, provoking questions and comments. For example:

- Will I be able to do this (collaboration) with practice and guidance?
- Most teachers aren't interested [in collaboration], some are very interested. I am in the middle of the road.
- I don't know if the rewards of collaboration will outweigh the time needed.
- I believe college credit was the driving force (motivation) that caused staff to come and stay in the project.

GETTING USED TO COLLABORATION

This project was being handled in a way that was very different from anything we had ever experienced. There was to be no leader; we were all in charge. We all had a say in the decisions and the direction of our school Quincentenary project. This was confusing for many, frightening for some, and downright exciting to others. This variety of responses is evident in the journals:

- When we started, we were so naive about how groups work without a designated leader. We did not know how to reach a consensus, nor was consensus even in our vocabulary.
- I was somewhat taken aback by the way the class was conducted. The idea and procedures of collaboration were new to me, and I left somewhat bewildered. Because of my flexibility and willingness to work with others, I remain open to this concept. I must say that it was really different. It's as if I found a whole new area of my thinking being stretched.
- Many of us were frustrated about Marilyn's being so vague.

Becoming leaders, making decisions together, and valuing multiple perspectives were things we had to learn in order to work collaboratively.

Competition in our school is an unspoken tension. In this collaborative project our competitive nature surfaced in many unexpected forms. We developed early on a sense of pride in our success in working together and felt competitive with the other schools. We were the first school to have an overall focus and plan designed. We had a sense of pride to be able to work successfully without help from the university. We made big plans for a flashy grandiose set of products that would put our school community and other project schools in awe of our expertise. We were so self-assured that we felt we knew everything. Marilyn came to an after-school meeting to hear about our plans, and we were angry when she dared to question the scope of our ideas.

- I'm glad we had the chance to share our ideas with Marilyn. For some reasons, though, I didn't feel her suggestions were accepted. I kind of felt like she was an outsider.
- We all seem to work, respect, flex so well together that I'm a little wary of newcomers.
- I was not happy to see Marilyn sitting in on our decision making. This is our project, not hers. As she reacted to our ideas, I wondered if she knew what she was doing. Marilyn came to the meeting with the stance of an expert, spent a minimal amount of time evaluating our long hours of work, questioned our goals, size, and theme of our project. She left us feeling confused, inadequate, and angry.

Marilyn's journal some days later described her feeling about her visit:

At this point in the project, I am having a difficult time defining my role. I am trying to encourage collaboration in the school groups and in the large group. In the beginning I had described the project as a joint venture between the schools and the university, but then there weren't enough university folks to be involved with each school. The Worthington group was the largest and had some strong leaders, so they ended up without an OSU person. Yet I felt I should give them some support, or at least know what was going on. When I went to the meeting at the school, I was excited to see everything that the group had done and their level of enthusiasm when they described their ideas. Yet I was fearful that they would become discouraged before they even began if they tried to do so much. In retrospect, I wished I had just asked questions, rather than give an opinion. I don't have a relationship yet established with the group, and I should have anticipated that I would be seen as an outsider.

We also felt a sense of superiority when teachers from other schools involved in the project asked for our advice. Our confident attitudes were well documented in several of our journal entries.

- I thought this woman [a teacher from another school group] came to speak to us because she felt we really knew what was expected—as if we were the "in-group." I could not help feeling a sense of superiority.

- When I look at how nervous and confused people get about making a decision in the other groups, it's no wonder they haven't gotten very far.

A spirit of cooperation within our group surfaced when we thought our ideas were being "stolen" by other schools. One of our group members was disgruntled when she realized that

> Our big ideas are being taken by other schools through our five-minute sharing time. [Each Thursday night meeting began with each school group sharing for five minutes.] If a school is going to steal a big idea, it should be borrowed—with permission from those who thought of the idea.

While most of us were horrified to think that our ideas might be used by others, one of our members remarked: "Isn't sharing ideas for everyone's benefit the essence of collaboration?" This teacher had previously worked collaboratively in another situation. She had experience in the process and understood some of what collaboration was about. The rest of us were only beginning to use the term. One member of our group wrote: "I'm anxious for our next get-together to collaborate more." Many of us were beginning to feel the same way. Collaboration was a new form of social contact that carried with it a sense of importance.

The possibility of participating in the city's Columbus Day parade provides another example of our competitive mind-set and also of our attitudes toward the socioeconomic differences among our schools. As the parade was discussed, there was some disagreement about who would participate. Many felt that if each school did not contribute financially in building our float, then their students should not be allowed to ride on it during the parade. The competitive nature of the issue became ugly, and feelings were hurt. The conflict was captured in a journal entry:

> Are we becoming a project of the haves versus the have-nots? Can the other schools generate the enthusiasm as strongly as our school from their staff and community, in particular, the parents of their school? With this possible situation of the haves versus the have-nots, will we be able to collaborate on equal terms for the rest of the project?

As usual, there was one wise person in our group who looked at this folly and reminded us, "It is important to remember the central core is collaboration, not competition." In the end the parade idea was dropped in favor of curricular activities that would support students' learning about the Quincentenary.

The question of our relationship to other schools came up occasionally. Was this project just a collection of individual schools doing different projects, or was there to be collaboration across the groups? The idea of a single project for all the schools came up at one point. The principals seemed to be in favor of this approach. As one teacher wrote:

> I wonder why the idea of all the schools working on a common project together appealed to the principals? Maybe they were interested in the PR it would bring to their schools. I don't think they have any idea what a mammoth undertaking this appeared to be to the teachers. If they had been present at all meetings [most principals attended only sporadically], they would have understood how much work and time that would involve. We are having enough trouble establishing trust and reaching a consensus in our small school groups.

At the end of the first quarter, one of the teachers created a metaphor to describe her perception of collaboration.

> When I think of our collaborative meetings, I am reminded of my washing machine. The actual outside structure represents OSU. It is the home of the process, of the idea. Marilyn is the laundress as she sets the setting. If there is only a little time, it goes on the minicycle; if we have lots of time, she turns the dial to the heavy-duty setting. Our core group is the laundry. We come to class limp and soiled with the grime of teaching. As we eat, chat, and listen to speakers, the tank is filled with water, soap, and appropriate additives. When our water level is up, the project sets us in motion. We start, for example, with Jeanna giving a playground report, and we all move around in that direction. When Mary then reminds us of the mural, we switch back in the opposite direction. We circulate back and forth among our various projects, back and forth, kachonk, kachonk. We have a sense of movement, but it is so circular we can't tell if there is any forward motion. Suddenly the project decides to take us for a fast spin, and we go in one direction and get a sense of accomplishment. Once again the tank fills and the project sets us in motion. In the end, we are cleaned and refreshed. We are interwoven and must be pulled apart to go our own separate ways.

PROBLEMS INSIDE OUR SCHOOL GROUP

Given our sense of superiority, it was only a matter of time before our competitive mode moved from an "us-versus-them" mentality to infighting among ourselves. By the second quarter, spring 1991, we had backed ourselves into a corner with a list of products that had deadlines. To complicate the picture, parents and community members were now involved in our plans. Previously, people were having conversations in the halls of our building to process weekly meetings or share new information. Now these same hallway discussions were used to seek approval for decisions made by one or two people. It seemed some folks were more comfortable with these kinds of negotiations than the collaborative process of the group meetings. These conversations could be viewed both positively and problematically. Positively, for the first time, we were having conversations about substantive issues. More communication between teachers was occurring than was typical for our building. The problem, however, was that we were beginning to take on the look of City Hall—there were more lobbyists working the halls than teachers.

PROCESS VERSUS PRODUCT

During spring quarter, our group splintered into what we called the "process" people and the "product" people. The process participants in our core group could not understand why everything had to be done so quickly, and the product-oriented participants insisted on deadlines. Some teachers took the initiative to do things that the core group had not decided on together. This came to a head when a couple of the teachers drafted a letter to be sent out to the parents in the name of the group, but the letter was not approved by the core group. It was complicated by the fact that there was a PTA project to build a new playground and some of us did not want the Quincentenary project to be confused with the PTA's project. There were heated conversations about the letter. One of the teachers who'd drafted the letter wrote:

> I am a person who usually takes the positive, bright side of things, but for once I feel like I got the bad end of the stick and that I was blamed for doing some things that I thought were right and good for our school.

In an effort to refocus on working collaboratively, the process-oriented participants argued for more talking and group decision making for all aspects of the project. We were convinced that even the most minute details needed to be decided by the group. This processing of all decisions was not acceptable to everyone. So in a rather uncollaborative fashion, some of us asked Marilyn, the university professor, to come remind the group that this project was a collaborative one. We should have predicted that bringing in the university professor, the person who traditionally holds the power, would cause more dissension within the group. One person captured this sense when she wrote, "When I saw Marilyn there, I was put on guard because I knew something was coming down." We made this same mistake of bringing in the "power person" several times. It took us some time to see the irony. On one hand, we were arguing for shared power, but whenever we did not get our way, we resorted to someone in a hierarchical role to support our position.

The following morning, one of the teachers called a meeting to confront Lisa and Rosario, the teachers in the research group who had invited Marilyn to the meeting. A meeting was held in the teachers' lounge. The teacher who called the meeting came with an agenda of items she wanted to discuss. The comments moved from the specifics of the agenda to more personal attacks. She felt the teachers in the research group were being dogmatic about imposing the process of collaboration on the entire group. She said she had not felt free to speak at the meeting with Marilyn because the tape recorder was on and the researchers controlled the meeting. The research group teachers (Lisa and Rosario) tried to clarify the issues from their point of view, but it was difficult. They had done a lot of talking about collaboration in the research group meetings. They had had time to struggle over issues with others and to gain from the experiences in the other schools. Because they had more insight about the process, some teachers expected them to provide direction. Others were jealous of the status of being in the research group and/or having the time to explore these issues more in depth. However, Lisa and Rosario were still novices and were unable to effectively communicate their knowledge verbally to the group. Because of this they were seen as elitist by other members of the school group. It was very tense at school, and many hurt feelings resulted.

A COMPROMISE

At the following day's meeting, the tone changed from dispute to compromise as we tried to define collaboration and come to some shared norms about how the group should make decisions. Each person shared his or her definition of collaboration. There were some common themes, including shared decision making, trust, a sense of ownership, and a commitment to communication. There was a plea to slow down the pace of our project, to facilitate the process, and to prioritize our goals. Members of the group requested that this meeting not be taped, so we do not have data from which to quote, but there are relevant journal entries about the activities of this week:

- Wow, what a week! I think this was a difficult experience, but I also think we learned an awful lot about collaboration.

- This week almost had to have happened!
- I regret that these divisions have occurred within the original [core] group. However, it was a learning experience for all of us! In any future effort to work in a collaborative manner, one should work to avoid this split and work toward a win/win situation and atmosphere.

While this was a helpful meeting, differences in the group continued. We continued fighting among ourselves, many hard feelings and heated discussions ensued, and two members of the product-oriented participants dropped out of the group. One teacher reflecting back on this time wrote:

> As I look back now, I can see that we thought we were all working together and "on the same page." However, we had no consensus as to how we were going to work together or what our goals were for the project. When we couldn't reach a consensus and people didn't agree, we started lobbying for support behind each others' backs. Compromise was at times for the benefit of the group and at other times for personal gain.

We continued to have many discussions about whether collaboration can work when a product is involved. Yet without a product, what reason would we have to collaborate? Most important, we asked ourselves, "Exactly what is collaboration?" Some in our group thought that to be collaborative, all decisions, no matter how trivial, should be brought back to the group for discussion. Others felt that since they had taken ownership of a segment of the project, they should have the right to make decisions they felt were appropriate. Journals during this time reflected many different attitudes:

- I still think we need to make decisions as a group so we can keep a sense of ownership.
- If people want to spring ahead to accomplish goals, that's okay.
- We have taken on things the group hasn't decided on. We could do the footwork, but we need to do the footwork the group has decided on.

We had read articles describing a collaborative process, so we knew a few things—collaboration is time consuming, requires trust among participants, and is a shared decision-making process. However, we were discovering that learning to be collaborative is not something you can learn by reading a book. It required "on-the-job training."

COLLABORATION TAKES TIME

During the spring quarter, the university invited proposals for professional development schools. It required a proposal that demonstrated ability to work collaboratively. The time line to submit a proposal was very short, and many of our group could not attend the open meetings to discuss this issue. The decision was made to submit a proposal even though most teachers, as well as Marilyn, were not sure what becoming a PDS would do to our school project. When our proposal was accepted late in the quarter, many of our teachers were disappointed because they thought it would interfere with the development of our Quincentenary school project.

We already had a week-long summer course planned that brought many speakers in to talk about issues related to the Quincentenary. To plan for the PDS, we needed to add another week. Many in our group wanted to work on our school project, but neither of these weeks allowed much time for school planning. Besides, people were in and out of town on vacations, so not everyone could be at either the Quincentenary class or the planning week. Nevertheless, those at the Quincentenary class met each day at lunch to talk about our project. Much of the discussion revolved around whether we could meet on Saturdays throughout the summer to work on the various parts of our school project. The issue kept festering because two people were unable or unwilling to attend the planning week where we could do a lot of group work.

A few members felt that it was crucial to meet our time table in order to satisfy parental expectations, so they argued for the Saturday meetings. We wanted credit for doing this planning, but Marilyn decided this was not legitimate. She was concerned that the whole group was not meeting and she anticipated problems because there were so many bad feelings.

During the lunchtime meetings, we also talked about negotiating a process for group decision making. We tried to define terms such as consensus, majority, quorum voting, and collaboration. The group struggled to decide whether to come to a group decision via consensus or majority rule, did we need a quorum to make any decisions, and how many members would make a quorum. One teacher wrote about the summer meetings:

> To me, the unsettling thing about the summer class were the sessions we had at lunchtime. Most sessions were somewhat tense. We were still in the stages of getting our programs and focus readied for the fall. The division in direction was quite evident [process versus product]. Marilyn met with us on one occasion and offered some direction, but still it seemed that we could not agree on the main focus. At one

meeting, a member of our staff, who was not a part of our school group, was present. Several comments were made and tempers flared [related to her participation in decision making]. This started more divisions in our school group about bringing new teachers into the project.

The next week was the planning meeting for the PDS and time for working on our Quincentenary projects. Three of our group were not able to attend, but the rest of the group spent the week developing a unit on perspective taking to lay the framework for appreciating different cultures. During the week, we also made many decisions about how to organize things for the 24 MEd students who would be assigned to our PDS in the fall. The students were already taking courses at the university, so some of them joined us for this planning. For most of us, this was the first time we had ever really thought about teacher education or had a chance to make decisions about field placements, supervision, and assignments for teacher education candidates. It took a lot of time because there were many decisions to make.

During the rest of the summer, our school group was unable to continue collaborative work on our project. Although we decided that we had no choice but to put the project on hold until fall, several members were insistent that these projects had to continue because parents were recruited and actively involved. So as a group we decided that these members could bring these projects to completion with our blessing, and we would abide by their decisions. They were asked not to attach the OSU Quincentenary project label to the projects.

These few members kept the entire group informed through phone calls and invitations to meetings. All who were interested were able to voice their opinion, yet few group members participated.

BEGINNING A NEW YEAR WITH NEW ISSUES

At our first WES staff meeting, held the day before school began, our collaborative group was on the agenda. Most of the core group was surprised to see our committee name on the agenda. There was a slight twist to the name, however. OSU had been deleted, with only the words "The Quincentenary" remaining.

At the same time, the core group learned that during the summer months a checking account was opened in the name of the WES Quincentenary project. There was more than $1,000 deposited in the account from revenue that came from the Worthington City Council and from the sale of T-shirts. The names of those authorized to sign checks included three non–core group members.

No one challenged the situation openly in order to avoid further conflict. There were, however, many hall conversations about who would have access and use of the money. Finally, a meeting was called to discuss the current situation, and Marilyn was invited.

We met after school in the computer room. Everyone came; the air was tense. To the surprise of the group, Marilyn led the meeting, stating that the Quincentenary project had begun with the core group and belonged to them and to OSU, period. Neither Marilyn's manner of handling the "collaborative" meeting nor her edict were challenged. Perhaps we were all too hurt and too tired to continue to battle with one another. In one way, we were glad to have the matter decided, yet in another it seemed we had regrettably gone back to the status quo of having a hierarchical figure make decisions for us.

Marilyn's journal reflects her point of view:

> This meeting was my third time to play the heavy. Did I have legitimate reasons for coming in and saying how it was going to be? At the time, it felt like the only choice if WES was going to continue as a group in a way that would fit in with the emerging norms of the larger group. The feelings were tense, the divisions clear, and now there were money issues and parent complaints. So after talking with the research group about the issues, I just went in and said how it was going to be—if there was to be identification and participation with the Quincentenary project, it had to be collaborative. What was unspoken was that it had to be collaborative in the way that I thought was collaborative, and the way one part of the group wanted it to go. We had, in a sense, conspired to place one part of the group's goals and choices ahead of the other.

As the school year began, we were working on our Quincentenary project plus supervising the new MEd interns and revising their university program. Keeping all this going was very difficult. Communication broke down. Frustration on all sides ensued. Our Thursday evening class meetings were spent mainly ironing out wrinkles in the PDS; there was seldom time to work on our Quincentenary project. New teachers from WES who had joined the group were rethinking their choice. Many core group teachers were not interested in the PDS issues and preferred to spend their time at school working on our Quincentenary project.

The PDS activities, particularly working with the MEd interns, required that we make decisions as a large group, not just within our school groups. We decided to have mixed school groups for discussion during our Thursday meetings. One of the byproducts of these meetings was a bonding with people from others schools. While we were trying to build a community, however, incidents occurred that alienated the WES group. On one Thursday night, one of the urban school principals began a lengthy monologue about how the job of suburban teachers was easier and therefore inferior. Only the "best" could and would accept the challenge of teaching in an urban setting. She defended her school's low test scores while belittling Worthington's higher scores. Other teachers and MEd interns present reacted initially with disbelief. This tirade served to alienate and divide the group just as we were moving toward feeling more like a group. In addition, we became gradually aware that the MEd interns preferred not to come to our school. Perhaps they thought us elitist, or perhaps they thought that they would not learn enough here to be prepared for the urban teaching jobs most likely available to them at graduation.

During the year at our school, four of the Project Group teachers began using the perspectives unit that we had developed during the summer. We shared this unit at a staff meeting and invited everyone to contribute ideas and time. We were proud of our product and excited to share it with the staff. We had already received feedback from students and parents regarding the unit and were pleased it had been so warmly received. Unfortunately, only a few teachers asked for a copy of the unit and no one other than core members used it in their classroom. In spite of our attempts, staff members did not seem to connect this unit to the essence of the Quincentenary.

PLANNING A SCHOOLWIDE PROJECT

During the year, we were also putting efforts into plans for an international night to be held in May. This would be the culmination of our Quincentenary projects. The theme, "Voyaging through the Americas," had been identified the previous spring and the idea of a school-wide festival had been discussed, but no specific plans had been made. We continued to work on ideas during Thursday night meetings when there was time.

As spring neared, we had many ideas, but none had been prioritized. One member of the core group who had experience with school-wide functions took the lead and called meetings that included our Project Group and any interested parents and staff. We discussed options, made decisions via a consensus, and set deadlines. With this common goal, we knew we had to work together and share the workload. Group members chose tasks, reported back to the group, the group made decisions, and progress ensued.

At this point in our project we seemed to be very productive and working well together. This was in sharp contrast to how things were the previous spring and summer. We were now focused on the process of collaboration as a way to achieve our Quincentenary goals, and we silently agreed to collaborate and be conscious of the process. We longed to return to the sense of community we had at the very beginning of the project, where people and different points of view were respected and valued. We were excited yet cautious, fearing a return to past conflicts.

We were concerned during the year about whether the rest of the WES staff would participate in the festival. This anxiety was accentuated by the fact that the Project Group had already alienated some staff members during our earlier stage of collaboration. Luckily, we were successful in recruiting at least one participant from each grade level (except kindergarten) to be a part of the Project Group for the winter and spring quarters to work on the festival. This facilitated communication. Soon there was a real momentum and the entire school was involved. International students visited classrooms, displays began to appear in classrooms and hallways, non–core group teachers attended Quincentenary group meetings, and the music teacher taught each grade level songs originating from its country of study.

The festival night was something to remember. Students, parents, and teachers all felt a sense of pride and camaraderie never before experienced in the history of our school, or ever since. Rooms were seeping with cultural wares, and students and parents turned out in great numbers. A mariachi band contributed to the spirit and authenticity of the evening. Our plans, dreams, and hard work were finally realized—it was a success![1]

As the evening ended, some staff members decided to go to a local restaurant to celebrate. Word was passed informally to other members of the Project Group and parent volunteers. Spontaneously a large group gathered at the restaurant for some "cheer."

The following Monday, some members of our staff were disgruntled. Some teachers felt slighted. They had worked hard and thought everyone should have been "invited." The core group discussed the problem and set up an after-school TGIF at a local Mexican restaurant. Parent volunteers and all staff members were invited. The celebration seemed a success, but whether the hurt feelings continued, we do not know.

In the spring during the festival planning we had twelve teachers in our group. By the next fall, only three teachers remained in the core group. Several who left were willing to share their reasons for not continuing:

- The goals of the group changed. We always talk about process, never focusing on the concrete.
- Now things have calmed down (group conflict), but I feel that if I had stayed with the group, conflict would have raged even more.
- I felt the collaborative group didn't back me up when it was needed.
- Since there is no goal at this time, I see no need to be a part of the collaborative group, even though I still enjoy working with all group members.

EXPANDING OUR FOCUS

The continuing three Project Group teachers attended the second summer planning week to get ready for the new cohort of MEd interns. We had learned a lot from things we tried with the students during the previous year and made many new plans. Whereas our previous collaborative project focused on a goal for our individual building, the new focus of the PDS was much broader—to change preservice teacher education and promote professional development for experienced teachers. Some teachers were interested in this focus, and others were not.

At this point in our case study, we are two years into our participation in the Quincentenary Project/PDS. As the research group changes its focus, work on collecting data for our case study stops, although our writing continues sporadically. In the research group, we have exhausted our focused study of collaboration and moved onto other interests and areas of action research.

ENDING THE STORY

In the following four years, there is continuing participation by several of the original Project Group, and other WES teachers come and go as their interests and time allow. The work of PDS continues as a separate track within the school. Except for the international festival project and a less successful attempt to do a school-wide festival in 1993, the Collaborative Project/PDS has not been integrated into the school in any sustained way. The three WES principals we have had over this six-year period have demonstrated varying degrees of support for PDS. Regardless of their varied support, the size and fragmentation within the school has not been conducive to integrating PDS, as was done in other PDS schools.

With hindsight, time, and distance from writing this case study, the conflicts have mellowed and what we gained is more apparent. We have learned that collaboration does not work for everyone. For years, the norms at WES were competitive rather than collaborative. Some teachers have goals and perspectives that do not support collaborative work. In trying to work collaboratively, we countered the established school norms. We learned how difficult it is to change these norms. We met very little success taking on the school as a whole. From our experience, we conclude that it takes time and perseverance to make a dent in an institutional system. It takes small groups of people working together, sometimes "going in the back door" to begin to create change.

Over time we have come to appreciate the value of sharing, both between ourselves and across schools. Many of us now value what we can learn from others. We have learned that competition isolates us rather than bringing us together. In a competitive mode, we miss the richness of what others outside the group can offer. This applies both to classroom practice and school projects.

In the beginning, we thought we had little to learn from teachers in urban settings, but they had much to learn from us. We have learned that while we each have some unique struggles and issues, we have many common concerns. We have learned much from our similarities as well as from our differences.

The process of writing this case study and then re-reading and editing it for the book has continued to support our reflection. We have learned much from our collaborative efforts, especially how difficult and valuable collaboration can be for professional development and growth.

NOTE

1. One of the outcomes of our successful school-wide project was that a number of individuals received recognition and awards from the school district and city. However, this too became a controversial issue. Some felt that no individual should be given recognition alone because it was a collaborative project, while others felt deserving of individual recognition.

Conclusion

We conclude this tale but not our collaboration. Our particular collaborative experiences are idiosyncratic, shaped by a context and set of personalities that are unlikely to be reproduced somewhere else. But our experience of talking to people in other collaborative projects leads us to believe that there are common themes and problems that we all face in breaking down the traditional barriers that have separated schools and universities.

Our vision of collaboration includes mutuality, caring relationships, and respect for our different expertise. As Vivian (1985) suggests:

> Collaboration arises from a recognition of mutual interest between school and college—between community and college—that must become widespread if we are to improve our public schools. Within a partnership of institutions there should be a coequal relationship of colleagues, a volunteer association of individuals who choose to work together, of allies in league to improve our schools. An equal importance must be attached to what each partner brings to the relationships. The aim is to work together without everybody changing places. (p. 87)

We began our collaborative project with mutual interests in several areas. First, we agreed to work collaboratively on a curricular project that seemed large at the time but paled by comparison as we assumed a PDS agenda. Our PDS agenda, tied to the Holmes Group initiatives, encompassed reform in schools, in teacher education, and at the university. Add to this a focus on urban education, and we were swimming in a sea of reform initiatives that piqued our imaginations and required everyone's expertise and best thinking.

Our approach initially was to work on this broad agenda piece by piece. We saw reform in teacher education, professional development, urban education, and inquiry (our four self-selected foci) as separate agenda items. The immediate needs of a cohort of MEd preservice students pressed us to pay attention to teacher education reform. We thought our own professional development would come later. We began an inquiry project to study collaboration as it unfolded in our various PDS schools, but this seemed detached from our teacher education efforts.

Slowly we came to see these separate aspects of our agenda as intricately intertwined and interdependent. As we learned more about collaboration, our work with preservice teachers and students in our classrooms became more collaborative (our inquiry informed our teacher education and teaching efforts). As we struggled to reform teacher education, we had to examine our own beliefs about good teaching and the institutional support/ constraints on teacher growth and empowerment (our teacher education efforts encouraged professional development). As we supervised preservice interns in our classrooms, they asked many questions and we were pushed to examine our beliefs and practices (teacher education informed our professional development).

The growing interdependence of our initially separate goals paralleled a growing understanding of our differences. The oft-cited conflicts between schools and universities were readily apparent in our beginning work together. Our institutional contexts socialize and reward us differently; we have different perspectives on many things. Our many hours together and time in each other's institutional contexts have created a level of understanding that we did not initially have. Clinical educator roles, co-teaching methods courses, and researching, writing, and presenting have helped us to understand the ways we are connected to our institutional contexts and to value the differences in perspective and expertise that we have.

Change and new understandings have seldom come easily. Even when we are positively predisposed to something new, there seems always to be doubt along the way. Sometimes the change goes smoothly but we run into peer disapproval or institutional barriers. Other times, the challenges are personal—too much ambiguity, too little predictability. Further, there is the perpetual tendency to slip back into the comfort zone—to do what is easier and safer. Sometimes, just when we think we have a handle on something, there are policy changes, funding reversals, and proposals denials, or classroom substitutes are canceled. Carefully nurtured relationships can be crushed by a harsh word or arbitrary decision made intentionally or unintentionally. Our previous stereotypes and prejudices readily reemerge as we perceive actions that conflict with the collaborative norms we have so recently co-constructed.

Yet change does occur. Many issues we struggled with in the beginning are rarely topics of conversation now—issues of power, intimidation, and lack of parity. We wonder sometimes if these issues have become invisible to us and are still problematic in ways that we do not find recognizable. Other times we revel in our accomplishments—the mutuality, strong relationships, and continued learning that occur in our group. As new people join us, we are puzzled about how to help them understand our history and shared values while at the same time allowing their perspectives to help us examine what we are doing and where we need to go.

The more we come to depend on this collaboration to nurture our professional development and reform initiatives, the more we doubt that these kinds of endeavors can be sustained. Will institutions in a time of tight resources and increased cries for accountability be able or willing to sustain this kind of bottom-up, time-intensive approach? Is it possible to document the value of these initiatives in ways that will convince administrators and politicians of their value? If we write truthful stories about the complexity, challenges, and problems of our work, will this interfere with gaining support? How long will people be willing to continue with the volunteer hours necessary to keep these projects operating when the prospect of adequate support to do the work during regular hours is not forthcoming? Will these endeavors remain small and elitist because of the expense and time requirements that exclude those with other personal or professional responsibilities during after-school hours?

For many of us, the lifeline to collaboration with others feels thin and tenuous. But the sustenance we receive from it belies its thin appearance. The changes in our thinking and practices, the reform in our schools, and the ways students are benefiting from our work are substantial. We are convinced daily that our professional lives have been directly affected by our collaboration with each other; we worry whether this change is sustainable if the support disappears. If policy makers are indeed committed to reform, if teachers' or professors' professional development is a key component in this change, if teacher education must change to meet the demands future teachers will face, and if schools and universities can no longer work separately to solve the complex problems that face us in schools today, we believe this kind of school/university collaboration is a viable approach to accomplishing these goals.

We offer our experience and reflections as a contribution to the discussion about the benefits and burdens of collaboration. We hope it will be provocative for those involved in similar work as well as convincing to policy makers to support this type of sustained long-term approach to educational reform and professional development. School/university collaboration will not solve all educational problems, nor is it the only way to effect reform. It is, however, a viable and integrative approach that has accomplished more than we ever intended and prompted change we could not have anticipated.

About the Author and Primary Contributors

Tom Adams has taught for 23 years in elementary grades. He has a BA in education from Indiana University of Pennsylvania and an MA degree from OSU. His master's project was a study of writing across the curriculum, focusing particularly on math portfolios. His primary interests are in multiple intelligences, educational uses of computers in the classroom, and math and writing portfolios. Tom has published in *Literacy Matters* (Adams, 1993). He has participated in the PDS since it began.

Mary Kathleen Barnes is currently a doctoral student at The Ohio State University with interests in literacy development, drama education, and teacher education and professional development. Her baccalaureate degree was in English and her MEd is in elementary education. Katie is currently working on a videotape series that is intended to improve student teacher observation skills. Katie works as a graduate associate in the PDS supervising MEd interns.

Reba Bricher has taught for 23 years with all but one year in the Columbus schools. She earned her undergraduate degree in education and completed her master's degree while participating in the PDS. She is particularly interested in the arts and education. She has published with Jean Tingley and Marilyn Hawk in *Teaching and Change* (Bricher, Hawk, & Tingley, 1990). Reba was a participant when the PDS began.

Mary Christenson's undergraduate degree in natural resources and agriculture was from Ohio State University. She has taught for 15 years in Minnesota and Ohio. For the last few years she has been doing action research in the area of cooperative learning with urban students. Her research will be published in *Teaching and Change* (Christenson & Serrao, 1997). She has a master's degree from Ohio State University and is currently working on a doctoral degree. She has participated in the PDS since it began and is published in *Theory Into Practice* (Christenson, Eldredge, Ibom, Johnston, & Thomas, 1996).

Don Cramer taught as an elementary teacher for 2 years, was a central office administrator for 10 years, and for 17 years worked as a building principal. For 3 years he was co-chair of the Ohio State University PDS Policy Board while also principaling. For 4 years he was a principal in one of our PDS schools.

Since his retirement he has worked at the university as program director for school/university partnerships. Don is particularly interested in what facilitates school reform, teacher leadership, and school/university partnerships.

Marilyn Hawk received her BA in education and psychology at Ashland University in Ohio and completed her master's degree at Ohio State University as part of her PDS involvement. She has taught kindergarten and first grade for 23 years in the Columbus schools and has particular interests in early literacy using activity and learning centers. She is a coauthor of an article in *Teaching and Change* (Bricher, Hawk, & Tingley, 1990) and has an article in *Literacy Matters* (Hawk, 1993).

Marilyn Johnston taught elementary school for 15 years while completing her MA in education and her PhD in the cultural foundation of education. She taught aesthetic education in the elementary education program at the University of Utah for seven years and now is associate professor of social studies and social foundations in the Department of Integrated Teaching and Learning at The Ohio State University. She is particularly interested in collaborative research, teacher development, and ways in which race, class, gender, and culture influence teaching and relationships within schools.

Richard Kerper taught for 15 years in elementary, middle, and high schools. For the last 4 years he has been an assistant professor, and he is now teaching at Millersville University in Pennsylvania. His major interests are in nonfiction literature for children, reader response to literature, and visual literacy. Rick is published in *Curriculum Inquiry* (Johnston & Kerper, 1996) and wrote chapters in *Young Adult and Public Libraries: A Handbook of Services and Materials* and *Handbook for Literacy Educators: Research on Teaching the Communicative and Visual Arts* (both Kerper, in press).

Kathleen Iböm has taught first and second grades for fifteen years. Her BA degree in education is from Indiana University, and she earned her MA while participating in the PDS. Her master's degree project was a collaborative, self-reflective study of her role as a clinical educator. Part of this study is published in *Theory Into Practice* (Christenson, Eldredge, Ibom, Johnston, & Thomas, 1996). Through the PDS she has become very interested in teacher change and the institutional constraints on professional development. Kathy is also interested in computer portfolios to track children's student progress. She has been a clinical educator in the PDS for three years.

Kathy Nalle has taught first, second, and third grades for 30 years. She worked as a reading specialist for 7 years. Kathy received a BA in education from

Bowling Green State University in Ohio and a master's degree from The Ohio State University. Kathy was in the original group that began the PDS, has co-taught science methods for MEd interns, and has supervised interns in her classroom. Her dream is to retire and write children's books. She has published articles describing her democratic approach to decision making in her classroom in *Teaching and Change* (1993) and *Teaching Tolerance* (1994).

Daa'iyah Saleem is currently a doctoral student at The Ohio State University, conducting her dissertation study looking at culturally specific notions of service learning as seen by administrators of service learning projects. She has professional interests in the social implications of technology, the value of service learning, and multicultural education, particularly as it relates to issues of spirituality. Before returning to the university for an MEd degree and certification, she worked for 8 years in private schools and then as an administrator for 3 years with Head Start programs.

Jean Tingley completed her undergraduate degree from The Ohio State University in business and then went back for certification in education after raising her children. She has taught for 11 years at Second Avenue Elementary. She completed a master's degree while participating in the PDS and is published in *Teaching and Change* (Bricher, Hawk, & Tingley, 1990).

J. Michael Thomas has taught middle school science, math, and gifted education for 14 years. He has a master's degree in future studies from the University at Houston at Clearlake and a PhD in educational administration with an emphasis in leadership and organizational change from The Ohio State University. Mike was our PDS ethnographer for 2 years and then became a full-time clinical educator/PDS co-coordinator. He does consulting in the area of using dialogue to promote organizational change.

Cynthia Tyson has taught kindergarten and first grade for 7 years in Columbus in a school with a math and environmental science focus. She then held a multicultural staff development position in the school district before returning to the university for a doctoral program. She did her undergraduate work in education at Youngstown State University in education and has a master's in education with reading certification from Ohio State University. Her primary interests are in multicultural education, with special focus on social activism and children's literature. She is currently completing a dissertation study on African American males' response to reality-based children's literature.

Lisa Westhoven taught third grade for 14 years at Worthington Estates Elementary, one of our PDS schools. She has taught gifted students and now has a full-inclusion classroom. Lisa completed her BA and MA degrees at Ohio State University. For 5 years she has been a co-coordinator of the PDS. She has particular interests in democratic classrooms and cooperative learning. For several years she has co-taught social methods courses for MEd interns. She has published in *Literacy Matters* (Westhoven, 1993).

Sue Wightman teaches kindergarten and first grade at Douglas Alternative Elementary School. She has taught for 28 years and has worked with many student teachers, including four of our PDS interns. She is particularly interested in early literacy and early childhood education.

PDS Publications and Conference Presentations

Bendau, S., Boyd, B., Ibom, K., Johnston, J., Johnston, M., Knecht, A., Mancus, D., Toderella, E., Underwood, D., & Westhoven, L. (1995, May). *A reader's theater performance: Learning from school/university collaboration.* Paper presented at the State of Ohio Professional Development School Conference, Athens, OH.

Boyd, B., Cordova, C., & Johnston, M. (1992, April). *Inquiry in an Ohio State University collaborative professional development school.* Paper presented at the First International Conference on Teacher Research, Stanford University, Palo Alto, CA.

Boyd, B., Gatto, K., Green, P., Johnston, M., & Westhoven, L. (1991, November). *Collaborative work as a moral endeavor: The influence of role.* Paper presented at the annual meeting of the Association for Moral Education, Athens, GA.

Boyd, B., Hohenbrink, J., Johnston, M., Sage, S., & Thomas, M. (1993, October). *Is it really collaborative when you can't find a parking place?* Paper presented at the Bergamo Conference, Dayton, OH.

Boyd, B., Hohenbrink, J., Johnston, M., Thomas, M., Swartz, M., Nalle, K., & Westhoven, L. (1993, May). *Collaborative supervision.* Paper presented at the The Ohio State University Research Conference, Columbus, OH.

Boyd, B., Hohenbrink, J., Johnston, M., & Westhoven, L. (1993, April). *Collaborative research on collaboration: Problems in working across school/university cultures.* Paper presented at the Second International Conference on Teacher Research, Athens, GA.

Boyd, B., Johnston, M., Saleem, D., Shorey, M., Thomas, M., & Westhoven, L. (1995, February). *School/university collaboration: Reframing and reconstructing our differences.* Paper presented at the Association of Teacher Education, Detroit, MI.

Burch, E., Cramer, D., Hernandez, A., Johnston, M., Loadman, B., Rentel, V., & Burke-Spero, R. (1995, February). *Using a professional development school model to restructure university–public school partnerships.* Paper presented at the American Association of Colleges of Teacher Education, Washington, DC.

Cramer, D., Dallmer, D., Johnston, M., & Moriarty, B. (1991, March). *A school university collaborative project to address controversial issues and the Columbian Quincentenary.* Paper presented at the annual meeting of the Association for Supervision and Curriculum Development, San Francisco, CA.

Dallmer, D., Harrison, D., Hohenbrink, J., Johnston, M., & Westhoven, L. (1991, October). *The influence of role in collaboration: First person narratives in a dialogue.* Paper presented at the annual meeting of the Mid-West Educational Research Association, Chicago, IL.

Dickins, C. (1994). *Too valuable to be rejected, too different to be embraced: A critical review of the literature on school/university collaboration* (Forum Paper No. 1). Columbus, OH: The Ohio State University, Professional Development School Publication Series.

Galarza, R., Green, P., Johnston, M., Kerper, R., Long, S., Smith, J., & Westhoven, L. (1991, May). *Collaborative research on collaboration.* Paper presented at the Ohio State University Research Conference, Columbus, OH.

Hohenbrink, J. (1993, February). *The influence of collaborative teaching.* Paper presented at the Association of Teacher Educators, San Francisco, CA.

Hohenbrink, J., Johnston, M., & Westhoven, L. (1992, November). *School and university perspectives on collaboratively teaching a social studies methods course: Three voices in a dialogue.* Paper presented at the College and University Faculty Assembly of the National Council for the Social Studies, Detroit, MI.

Hohenbrink, J., Johnston, M., Westhoven, L., with, Bossard, K., Dove, T., Merryfield, M., & Rayburn, B. (1994, November). *Learning from our teaching: Co-teaching social studies methods courses.* Paper presented at the College and University Faculty Assembly of the National Council of the Social Studies, Phoenix, AZ.

Johnston, M. (1996, July). *School/university collaboration: Unexpected outcomes.* Paper presented at the Second International Conference on Teacher Education, Tel Aviv, Israel.

Johnston, M., & Kerper, R. (1992, April). *School/university collaboration: The influence of role.* Paper presented at the annual meeting of the American Educational Research Association, San Francisco, CA.

Johnston, M., & Kerper, R. (Eds.). (1993). *School/university collaboration: Collaboration, collegiality, and change* (Vol. 5). Columbus, OH: The Martha L. King Language and Literacy Center at The Ohio State University.

Johnston, M., & Kirschner, B. (Eds.). (1996). *The Challenges of School/University Collaboration* (Vol. 35). Columbus, OH: The College of Education, The Ohio State University.

Johnston, M., & Thomas, M. (1994). *School and university collaboration: Can we reframe our differences?* (Forum Paper No. 4). Columbus, OH: The Ohio State University, Professional Development School Publication Series.

Johnston, M., & Thomas, M. (1995, April). *Teachers and professors changing roles: Expected and unexpected outcomes.* Paper presented at the American Educational Research Association, San Francisco, CA.

Saleem, D. (1995). *Service learning in PDSs: Personal experience and cultural traditions in African American culture* (Forum Paper No. 5). Columbus, OH: The Ohio State University, Professional Development School Publication Series.

See References for other PDS publications, including Adams, 1993; Bricher, Hawk, & Tingley, 1990; Christenson, Eldredge, Ibom, Johnston, & Thomas, 1996; Christenson & Serrao, 1997; Hawk, 1993; Johnston & Kerper, 1996; Johnston, 1994; Nalle, 1993, 1994; Westhoven, 1993.

References

Adams, T. (1993). A collaborative adventure. *Literacy Matters, 5*(2), 5-9.

Apple, M. (1986). *Teachers and texts: A political economy of class and gender relations in education.* New York: Routledge & Kegan Paul.

Barth, R. (1990). *Improving schools from within.* San Francisco, Jossey-Bass.

Benjamin, W. (1968). *Illuminations* (H. Zohn, Trans.). New York: Schocken.

Bohm, D. (1996). *On dialogue.* Lee Nichol (Ed.). New York: Routledge & Kegan Paul.

Bourdieu, P. (1977). *Outline of a theory of practice.* Cambridge: Cambridge University Press.

Bricher, R., Hawk, M., & Tingley, J. (1990). Cross-age tutoring for at-risk students. *Teaching and Change, 1*(1), 91-97.

Britzman, D. (1991). *Practice makes practice: A critical study of learning to teach.* Albany: State University of New York Press.

Butler, J. (1992). Contingent foundations: Feminism and the question of postmodernism. In J. Butler & J. Scott (Eds.), *Feminists theorize the political.* New York: Routledge.

Butler, J. (1993). *Bodies that matter: On the discursive limits of sex.* New York: Routledge.

Carnegie Forum on Education and the Economy. (1986). *A nation prepared: Teachers for the 21st century.* New York: Author.

Cherryholmes, C. (1988). *Power and criticism: Post-structural investigations in education.* New York: Teachers College Press.

Christenson, M., Eldredge, F., Ibom, K., Johnston, M., & Thomas, M. (1996). Collaboration in support of change. *Theory Into Practice, 35*(3), 187-195.

Christenson, M., & Serrao, S. (Winter, 1997). Cooperative learning in a hostile environment. *Teaching and Change, 4*(2), 137-156.

Clift, R. T., Veal, M. L., Holland, P., Johnson, M., & McCarthy, J. (1995). *Collaborative leadership and shared decision making.* New York: Teachers College Press.

Collins, J. L. (1995). Listening but not hearing: Patterns of communication in an urban school-university partnership. In H. G. Petrie (Ed.), *Professionalization, partnership and power: Building professional development schools* (pp. 77-92). Albany, New York: State University of New York Press.

Connolly, W. E. (1991). *Identity/difference: Democratic negotiations of political paradox.* Ithaca, NY: Cornell University Press.

Cryns, T., & Johnston, M. (April, 1993). A collaborative case study of teacher change: From a personal to a professional perspective. *Teaching and Teacher Education, 9*(2), 148-158.

Cryns, T., Hunsaker, L., Johnston, M., Warshow, L., & Weight, H. (1990). Lessons on relating research, reflection and reform from three researcher/practitioner projects. Paper presented at the American Educational Research Association, New York, NY.

Darling-Hammond, L. (1994). *Professional development schools: Schools for developing a profession*. New York: Teachers College Press.

Davies, B., & Harré, R. (1990). Positioning: The discursive production of selves. *Journal for the Theory of Social Behavior, 20*(1), 43–63.

Derrida, J. (1989). Structure, sign and play in the discourse of the human sciences. In D. Richter (Ed.), *Classical texts and contemporary trends* (pp. 959–971). New York: St. Martin's.

Dewey, J. (1916). *Democracy and education*. New York: Macmillan.

Dewey, J. (1984). *The Public and Its Problems*. Carbondale, IL: Southern Illinois University Press. (Originally published in 1927)

Elbow, P. (1986). *Embracing contraries: Explorations in learning and teaching*. New York: Oxford University Press.

Fine, M. (Ed.). (1992). *Disruptive voices: The possibilities of feminist research*. Ann Arbor: University of Michigan Press.

Foucault, M. (1978). The history of sexuality (R. Hurley, Trans.). New York: Pantheon.

Gadamer, H. G. (1976). *Philosophical hermeneutics*. Berkeley: University of California Press.

Gadamer, H. (1984). *Truth and method* (G. Barden & J. Cummings, Trans.). New York: Crossroads.

Greene, M. (1988). Reflection and passion in teaching. *Journal of Curriculum and Supervision, 2*(1), 68–81.

Greene, M. (1995). *Releasing the imagination: Essays on education, the arts and social change*. San Francisco: Jossey-Bass.

Haberman, M. (1971). Twenty-three reasons why universities can't educate teachers. *Journal of Teacher Education, 22*, 133–140.

Haraway, D. (1988). Situated knowledges: The science question in feminism and the privilege of partial perspective. *Feminist Studies, 14*(3), 575–599.

Hardford, M. (1987). *Where's Waldo?* Boston: Little, Brown.

Hawk, M. (1993). Collaborating with colleagues. *Literacy Matters, 5*(2), 10–14.

Heckman, P. (1988). The Southern California Partnership: A retrospective analysis. In K. Sirotnik & J. Goodlad (Eds.), *School-university partnerships in action* (pp. 106–123). New York: Teachers College Press.

Henderson, J. G., & Hawthorne, R. E. (Eds.). (1995). *The dialectics of creating professional development schools*. Albany, New York: State University of New York Press.

Hohenbrink, J. (1993). *The influence of collaboratively teaching a social studies methods course: University and school*. Unpublished dissertation, The Ohio State University, Columbus, OH.

Hohenbrink, J., Johnston, M., & Westhoven, L. (1992, November). *School and university perspectives on collaboratively teaching a social studies methods course: Three voices in a dialogue*. Paper presented at the College and University Faculty Assembly of the National Council for the Social Studies, Detroit, MI.

Hohenbrink, J., Johnston, M., & Westhoven, L. (in press). Challenges and changes: Collaborative teaching of a social social studies methods course. *Journal of Teacher Education*.

Holmes Group. (1986). *Tomorrow's teachers: A report of the Holmes Group*. East Lansing, MI: Author.

Holmes Group. (1990). *Tomorrow's schools: Principles for the design of professional development schools*. East Lansing, MI: author.

Holmes Group. (1995). *Tomorrow's schools of education: A report of the Holmes Group*. East Lansing, MI: author.

hooks, b. (1994). *Teaching to transgress*. New York: Routledge.

Howey, K., & Zimpher, N. (1989). *Profiles of preservice teacher education: Inquiry into the nature of programs*. Albany, NY: State University of New York Press.

Hunsaker, L., & Johnston, M. (1992). Teacher under construction: A collaborative case study of teacher reflection and change. *American Educational Research Journal, 29*(2), 350-372.

Isaacs, W. N. (1993). Taking flight: Dialogue, collective thinking, and organizational learning. *Organizational Dynamics, 2*(2), 24-39.

Johnston, M. (April, 1991). Ethical problems in three qualitative studies of teachers. Paper presented at the annual meeting of the American Educational Research Association, Chicago, IL.

Johnston, M. (Summer/Fall, 1994). Postmodern consideration of school/university collaboration. *Teaching Education, 6*(2), 99-106.

Johnston, M., & Kerper, R. M. (1996). Positioning ourselves: Parity and power in collaborative work. *Curriculum Inquiry, 26*(1), 5-24.

Knight, S. L., Wiseman, D., & Smith, C. W. (1992). The reflectivity-activity dilemma in school-university partnerships. *Journal of Teacher Education, 43*(3), 269-277.

Lakoff, G., & Johnson, M. (1980). *Metaphors we live by*. Chicago: University of Chicago Press.

Lampert, M. (1991). Looking at restructuring from within a restructured role. *Phi Delta Kappan*, 670-674.

Lather, P. (1989). Postmodernism and the politics of enlightenment. *Educational Foundations, 3*(3), 7-28.

Lather, P. (1996). *Methodology as subversive repetition: Practices toward a feminist double science*. Paper presented at the American Education Research Association, New York, NY.

Lather, P., & Smithies, C. (1995). *Troubling angels: Women living with HIV/AIDS*. Columbus, OH: Greyden Press.

Leach, M. (1994/1995). (Re)searching Dewey for feminist imaginaries: Linguistic continuity, discourse, and gossip. *Studies in Philosophy and Education, 13*, 291-306.

McRobbier, A. (1982). The politics of feminist research: Between talk, text, and action. *Feminist Review, 12*, 46-59.

Miller, L. (1995). *Professional development schools: Linking school renewal and teacher education*. Paper presented at the First International Conference on Teacher Education: From practice to theory, Tel Aviv, Israel.

Minh-ha, T. (1989). *Woman/native/other*. Bloomington, IN: Indiana University Press.

Nalle, K. (1993). Democratic processing of children's classroom concerns. *Teaching and Change, 1*(1), 25-54.

Nalle, K. (1994, Fall). A democracy of third graders. *Teaching Tolerance, 3*(2), 54-57.

Newman, S. (1989). *Worldwalk: One man's four-year journey around the world*. New York: Avon Books.

Nicholson, L. J. (1990). *Feminism/postmodernism*. New York: Routledge.

Nisbet, R. (1970). *The social bond*. New York: Knopf.

Noddings, N. (1984). *Caring*. Berkeley: University of California Press.

Oakley, A. (1981). Interviewing women: A contradiction in terms. In H. Roberts (Ed.), *Doing feminist research*. London: Routledge & Kegan Paul.

Petrie, H. G. (Ed.). (1995). *Professionalization, partnership, and power: Building professional development schools*. Albany, New York: State University of New York Press.

Rich, A. (1993). *The dream of a common language: Poems 1974-1977*. New York: W. W. Norton.

Richardson, L. (1995). Writing: A method of inquiry. In N. Denzin & Y. Lincoln (Eds.), *Handbook of Qualitative Research* (pp. 516-529). Thousand Oaks, CA: Sage.

Rogoff, B., Turkanis, C., & Bartlett, L. (Eds.). *A community of learners*. Oxford, England: Oxford University Press, in press.

Schratz, M., & Walk, R. (1995). *Research as social science*. London: Routledge & Kegan Paul.

Senge, P. M. (1990). *The fifth discipline: The art and practice of the learning organization*. New York: Doubleday.

Sirotnik, K. A., & Goodlad, J. I. (Eds.). (1988). *School-university partnerships in action: Concepts, cases, and concerns*. New York: Teachers College Press.

Spivak, G. (Ed.). (1988). *Can the subaltern speak?* Urbana, IL: University of Illinois Press.

Stanley, L., & Wise, S. (1983). *Breaking out: Feminist consciousness and feminist research*. London: Routledge and Kegan Paul.

Stoddart, T. (1995). The professional development school: Building bridges between cultures. In H. G. Petrie (Ed.), *Professionalization, partnership and power: Building professional development schools* (pp. 41-59). Albany, NY: State University of New York Press.

Symonds, P. M. (1958). An educational interest inventory. *Educational and Psychological Measurements, 18*(2), 377-385.

Van Maanen, J. (1988). *Tales of the field: On writing ethnography*. Chicago: University of Chicago Press.

Visweswaran, K. (1994). *Fictions of feminist ethnography*. Minneapolis: University of Minnesota Press.

Vivian, J. R. (1985). Empowering teachers as colleagues: The Yale-New Haven teachers institute. In W. T. Daley (Ed.), *College-school collaboration: Appraising the major approaches* (pp. 78-99). San Francisco: Jossey-Bass.

Weedon, C. (1987). *Feminist practice and post-structuralist theory*. London: Basil Blackwell.

Westhoven, L. (1993). Swimmy: A role model. *Literacy Matters, 5*(2), 2-5.

Winitsky, N., Stoddart, T., & O'Keefe, P. (1992). Great expectations: Emergent professional development schools. *Journal of Teacher Education, 43*(1), 3-18.

Zeichner, K. (1991). Contradictions and tensions in the professionalization of teaching and the democratization of schools. *Teachers College Record, 92*(3), 363-379.

Zimpher, N. (1990). Creating professional development school sites. *Theory into Practice, 29*(1), 42-49.

Index